# Exploring Japan
## Visiting and Talking about World Heritage Sites in Japan

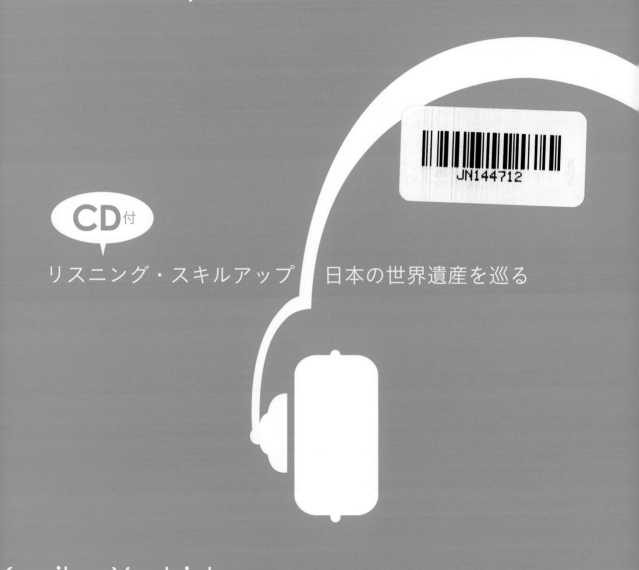

CD付

リスニング・スキルアップ　日本の世界遺産を巡る

Kuniko Yoshida

Masashi Hidaka

Harry Kearns

Azusa Yamamoto

SANSHUSHA

## 音声ダウンロード&ストリーミングサービス(無料)のご案内

http://www.sanshusha.co.jp/onsei/isbn/9784384334432/

本書の音声データは、上記アドレスよりダウンロードおよびストリーミング再生ができます(付属CDと内容は同じです)。ぜひご利用ください。

写真提供

Introduction　園部孝夫、ショーン・イワサワ、吉田国子
Unit 1　阿部達、吉田国子、日本コカ・コーラ株式会社、カゴメ株式会社、大関株式会社
Unit 2　園部孝夫、ハリー・カーンス、吉田国子
Unit 3　飯泉明男、園部孝夫、吉田国子
Unit 4　吉田国子
Unit 5　吉田国子
Unit 6　園部孝夫、吉田国子
Unit 7　©JFA、吉田国子
Unit 8　日本美術刀剣保存世協会、吉田国子
Unit 9　広島平和記念資料館所蔵・提供（撮影者・作者：川原四儀、小松キクエ）、吉田国子
Unit 10　園部孝夫、吉田国子
Unit 11　阿部達、園部孝夫、大塚製薬株式会社
Unit 12　金林卓哉
Epilogue　吉田国子

# はじめに

本書『Exploring Japan—Visiting and Talking about World Heritage Sites in Japan リスニング・スキルアップ：日本の世界遺産を巡る』は、リスニング力とスピーキング力の増進を目指す皆さんのための教材です。アメリカ人のライターであるヘンリーが日本人のアシスタントのエミと共に日本の世界遺産を訪ね、日本の文化に触れていきます。

本書は Introduction から始まり 12 のユニットを経て Epilogue で終わる 14 課の構成になっています。各ユニットには、Warm-up, Conversation 1, Background information, Conversation 2 の4つのリスニングセクションと、Vocabulary と Useful Expressions があり、聞き取り練習を行った後でそのユニットで出てきた単語の学習と表現の練習ができるようになっています。各ユニットの仕上げとして Quiz があり、単語の定着を確認して次のユニットへ進むようになっています。また、巻末には Extra activities としてリスニングの穴埋め問題と会話練習の発展問題を掲載しています。

本書の英文は4名の著者によるオリジナルです。日本の世界遺産を舞台にした内容であるため、歴史的建造物や歴史上の人物のこともたくさん出てきます。皆さんに身近に感じていただけると思っています。また皆さんが本書を通して日本各地の良さを再発見し、日本の文化を英語で表現する方法を学んでくださることを期待しています。

本書作成にあたって、多くの方々にご協力いただきました。写真をご提供くださった皆様、広島原爆資料館、日本美術刀剣保存協会、阿部達氏、飯泉明男氏、金林卓哉氏、ショーン・イワサワ氏に深く感謝いたします。また写真の撮影や図版の加工では園部孝夫氏に、編集・校正では三修社編集部の菊池暁氏と山本拓氏に大きなご助力をいただきました。ここに改めて謝意を表します。

著者代表　吉田国子

追記
本書に記載されている世界遺産は 2014 年までに登録されたものです。2022 年9月現在、下記のものが新たに登録されています。
- Sites of Japan's Meiji Industrial Revolution: Iron and Steel, Shipbuilding and Coal Mining（明治日本の産業革命遺産 製鉄・鉄鋼、造船、石炭産業、2015 年）
- The Architectural Work of Le Corbusier, an Outstanding Contribution to the Modern Movement（ル・コルビュジエの建築作品—近代建築運動への顕著な貢献、2016 年）
- Sacred Island of Okinoshima and Associated Sites in the Munakata Region（「神宿る島」宗像・沖ノ島と関連遺産群、2017 年）
- Hidden Christian Sites in the Nagasaki Region（長崎と天草地方の潜伏キリシタン関連遺産、2018 年）
- Mozu-Furuichi Kofun Group: Mounded Tombs of Ancient Japan（百舌鳥・古市古墳群—古代日本の墳墓群—、2019 年）
- Jomon Prehistoric Sites in Northern Japan（北海道・北東北の縄文遺跡群、2021 年）
- Amami-Oshima Island, Tokunoshima Island, Northern part of Okinawa Island, and Iriomote Island（奄美大島、徳之島、沖縄島北部及び西表島、2021 年）

# Contents

Introduction — 5

Unit 1　Shiretoko　知床 — 10

Unit 2　Shrines and Temples of Nikko　日光の社寺 — 14

Unit 3　Ogasawara Islands　小笠原諸島 — 18

Unit 4　Historic Villages of Shirakawa-go and Gokayama　白川郷・五箇山の合掌造り集落 — 22

Unit 5　Historic Monuments of Ancient Kyoto　古都京都の文化財 — 26

Unit 6　Historic Monuments of Ancient Nara　古都奈良の文化財 — 30

Unit 7　Sacred Sites and Pilgrims Routes in the Kii Mountain Range　紀伊山地の霊場と参詣道 — 34

Unit 8　Himeji-jo　姫路城 — 38

Unit 9　Hiroshima Genbaku Dome　原爆ドーム — 42

Unit 10　Itsukushima Shinto Shrine　厳島神社 — 46

Unit 11　Yakushima　屋久島 — 50

Unit 12　Gusuku Sites and Related Properties of the Kingdom of Ryukyu　琉球王国のグスク及び関連遺産群 — 54

Epilogue — 58

Extra activities — 61

# Introduction

## Warm-up

**1** Listen to the recording and choose the statement that best describes each photo.

写真の説明文を聞いて、最も適切なものをA〜Dから選びましょう。

(1) _____    (2) _____

## Conversation 1

Henry Wilckens, a writer for a travel magazine, has just arrived at Kansai International Airport in Japan and is meeting his assistant Emiko Takahashi.

**2** Listen to Conversation 1. Fill in the chart with appropriate answers.

会話1を聞いて、表を完成させましょう。

| What is his name? | |
|---|---|
| What does he do? | |
| Where did he come from? | |
| Why did he come to Japan? | |
| How does he feel now? | |

| What is her name? | |
|---|---|
| What is her nickname? | |
| What is she trying to do? | |
| What will she do now? | |

**3** Listen to Conversation 1 again and answer the questions.

会話1をもう一度聞いて、質問に英語で答えましょう。

(1) What will they do tomorrow?
(2) What time will they do it?

Introduction

## Background information

**4** Listen to the background information and choose the right one.

音声を聞いて、(　　　)の中の正しい語句を選びましょう。

(1) World Heritage sites are chosen by (UNESCO / UNICEF).
(2) World Heritage sites are (critically or economically / culturally or environmentally) important places.
(3) As of 2013, (901 / 981) sites are listed in (116 / 160) countries.
(4) World Heritage sites are supported with money from the (World Heritage Fund / World Heritage Band).
(5) Japan was awarded its first World Heritage sites in (1996 / 1993).

**5** Look at the list of the World Heritage sites in Japan. Match the number to the pictures on the map.

下記は日本の世界遺産のリストです。次ページの地図に正しい番号を入れましょう。

❶ Horyuji Temple
❷ Himeji-jo
❸ Monuments of Ancient Kyoto
❹ Shirakawa-go and Gokayama
❺ Hiroshima Genbaku Dome
❻ Itsukushima Shinto Shrine
❼ Monuments of Ancient Nara
❽ Shrines and Temples of Nikko
❾ Gusuku Sites and Related Properties of the Kingdom of Ryukyu
❿ Sacred Sites and Pilgrims Routes in the Kii Mountain Range
⓫ Iwami Ginzan Silver Mine and its Cultural Landscape
⓬ Historic Sites and Monuments of Hiraizumi
⓭ Yakushima
⓮ Shirakami Sanchi
⓯ Shiretoko
⓰ Ogasawara Islands
⓱ Fujisan
⓲ Tomioka Silk Mill and Related Sites

## Conversation 2

Henry and Emi are riding in the taxi to the hotel and are having a discussion about what parts of Japanese culture they like.

**6** Listen to Conversation 2. Check the items Henry and Emi like. Write H for Henry and E for Emi. Some items are liked by both Henry and Emi.

会話2を聞いて、ヘンリーが好きなものにはH、エミが好きなものにはE、二人とも好きなものにはHとEを下線部に書きましょう。

 (1) _____   (2) _____   (3) _____   (4) _____   (5) _____

 (6) _____   (7) _____   (8) _____   (9) _____   (10) _____

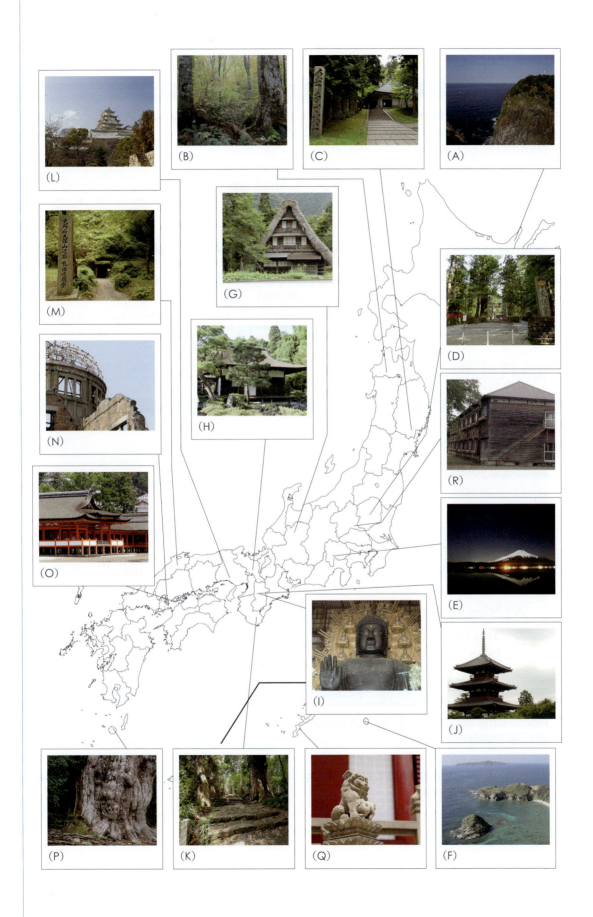

# Introduction

## Vocabulary

### Japanese things

Brainstorm some vocabulary necessary for introducing Japanese culture. Think of some Japanese words and then find their meaning in English.

日本文化を紹介するために必要な単語を学習しましょう。

| temple | shrine | forest | lake | martial arts | hot spring | tea ceremony |

他に必要な単語を日本語で書き出してその英訳を調べましょう。

### Self- introduction

Brainstorm some vocabulary necessary for a self-introduction. Write down your ideas in Japanese and then find their meaning in English.

自己紹介に必要な単語を日本語で書き出してその英訳を調べましょう。所属大学、学部、学科名など、正式な英語名称も調べましょう。

## Useful Expressions

### Self- introduction

Practice the self-introduction expressions you have learned.
自己紹介の表現を練習しましょう。

**Introduce yourself to your partner.**
パートナーに自分のことを紹介しましょう。

ex. A : Hello. I'm ……… of （所属学科など）/ from （出身地、出身高校など）
　　B : Hi. My name is ………….
　　　　Sorry, I didn't catch your name. Could you say that again?

　　A : Nice to meet you, …………
　　B : You can call me ……….
　　A : I see. Please call me ………..

### Likes and dislikes

Practice the likes and dislikes expressions.
好き、嫌いの表現を練習しましょう。

**Think of three things you like and how much you like them. Start a conversation expressing how much you like something. Try to keep the conversation going by replying to your partner's likes.**

好きな食べ物 / 有名人 / 映画・歌などをそれぞれ３つ思い浮かべましょう。それがどれくらい好きか考え、適切な表現を使って会話を始めましょう。相手が言ったものに対する自分の好みを伝えて会話を続けましょう。

ex. A : I'm crazy about chocolate.
　　　Do you like it?
　B : Yes, I love chocolate!
　　　No, I don't like chocolate very much.
　　　I like potato chips better.

　A : Haruki Murakami is fantastic.
　　　What do you think of him?
　B : I'm very keen on his novels, too.
　　　Well, I think he is OK. But I don't read books much.
　　　I like Manga a lot.

| | |
|---|---|
| I'm crazy about … <br> … is fantastic./ I love … | like  |
| I'm very keen on … <br> I like … very much (a lot). | |
| I like …… / I enjoy … <br> I think … is not bad. | |
| I think … is OK. <br> … makes me feel uneasy. | |
| I don't like … very much. <br> I hate … | dislike |

# Unit 1  Shiretoko

## 🎧 Warm-up

**1** Listen to the recording and choose the statement that best describes each photo.

写真の説明文を聞いて、最も適切なものを A～D から選びましょう。

(1) _____

(2) _____

## 🎧 Conversation 1

Henry and Emi are heading to Tokyo to take their flight to Shiretoko. It is the first time for Henry to ride on a bullet train.

**2** Listen to Conversation 1. Check the items Henry and Emi bought.
Write H for Henry and E for Emi. Some items may be bought by both Henry and Emi.

会話 1 を聞いて、ヘンリーが買ったものに H、エミが買ったものに E を下線部に書きましょう。

(1) _____   (2) _____   (3) _____   (4) _____   (5) _____   (6) _____

(7) _____   (8) _____   (9) _____   (10) _____   (11) _____

**3** Listen to Conversation 1 again. Which is the receipt Henry and Emi will receive?

会話1をもう一度聞いて、ヘンリーとエミが受け取るレシートの番号に○をつけましょう。

| (1) _____ | |
|---|---|
| Japan Diner | |
| 2014年6月13日 | |
| 0011　サンドイッチ　　1 | 300 |
| 0016　茶　　　　　　　2 | 300 |
| 0009　おにぎり　　　　2 | 300 |
| 小計　　　　　　　　 5点 | 900 |
| 現計 | 900 |
| お預り | 900 |
| おつり | 0 |

| (2) _____ | |
|---|---|
| Japan Diner | |
| 2014年6月13日 | |
| 0011　サンドイッチ　　1 | 300 |
| 0016　茶　　　　　　　2 | 300 |
| 0009　おにぎり　　　　1 | 150 |
| 小計　　　　　　　　 4点 | 750 |
| 現計 | 750 |
| お預り | 750 |
| おつり | 0 |

| (3) _____ | |
|---|---|
| Japan Diner | |
| 2014年6月13日 | |
| 0011　サンドイッチ　　2 | 600 |
| 0016　茶　　　　　　　2 | 300 |
| 0009　おにぎり　　　　1 | 150 |
| 小計　　　　　　　　 5点 | 1050 |
| 現計 | 1050 |
| お預り | 1050 |
| おつり | 0 |

| (4) _____ | |
|---|---|
| Japan Diner | |
| 2014年6月13日 | |
| 0011　サンドイッチ　　1 | 300 |
| 0016　茶　　　　　　　1 | 150 |
| 0009　おにぎり　　　　1 | 150 |
| 0030　日本酒　　　　　1 | 300 |
| 小計　　　　　　　　 4点 | 900 |
| 現計 | 900 |
| お預り | 1000 |
| おつり | 100 |

## Background information

**4** Listen to the background information. Complete the chart about Shiretoko National Park.

音声を聞いて、知床国立公園について表を完成させましょう。

| Location | |
|---|---|
| Origin of the word "Shiretoko" | |
| Designated year | |
| Famous for | Beautiful spruce and fir forests |

# Unit 1 Shiretoko

## Conversation 2

Henry and Emi are visiting an Ainu museum.

**5** Listen to Conversation 2. Read the statements and write T if the statement is true and write F if the statement is false.

会話2を聞いて、(1) ～ (5) の英文が会話の内容と合っていればT、合っていなければFを（　　）に書きましょう。

(1) The Ainu and the Japanese are different people.　　(　　)
(2) There are no Ainu left in Japan.　　(　　)
(3) Men wore tattoos around their lips and on their arms.　　(　　)
(4) Women never had their hair cut after a certain age.　　(　　)
(5) There are places where people can learn about Ainu culture.　(　　)

**6** Listen to Conversation 2 again. Answer the questions.

会話2をもう一度聞いて、質問に英語で答えましょう。

(1) What do some scholars think about the Ainu?
(2) Besides Japan, where else do Ainu people live?

## Vocabulary

### Verbs typically used for asking and giving permission

**Learn verbs typically used for asking and giving permission.**

許可を求める、与える表現の中でよく使われる動詞を学習しましょう。動詞の後にどのような語句がくるかを考えましょう。

```
borrow    cancel    download    join    leave    order    propose    postpone    publish
return    send      submit      sit     talk/tell  upload   use        quit         wait
```

### Food and drinks you may order at a KIOSK or other places

**Learn food and drink vocabulary.**

駅の売店、電車の中、スナックスタンドなどで買える飲食物に関係する語句を学習しましょう。

```
tomato juice   green tea   sandwich   chocolate   beverage   coffee   water   hamburger
French fries   gum   candies   potato chips   a can/two cans of …   a bottle/two bottles of …
a bag/two bags of …    a cup/two cups of …    a pack of/two packs of …
```

## Useful Expressions

### Asking and giving permission

**Practice expressions for asking and giving permission. Use the vocabulary you learned in the previous section.**

許可を求める、与える表現を練習しましょう。Vocabulary セクションで学習した単語を使って、会話をしましょう。

ex. A: May I sit by the window?
　　B: Sure. / Yes, go ahead. / Of course. Feel free to …
　　　 Sorry, but you can't. The seat is taken.
　　　 I'm sorry, but I'm afraid this seat is taken.

　　A: Is it OK if I cancel our appointment for tomorrow?
　　B: OK, I don't mind.
　　　 No, tomorrow is the only day I'm free.

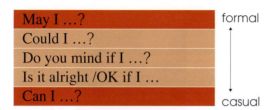

## Ordering food

Practice expressions for ordering food. Use the vocabulary you learned in the previous section.

Vocabulary セクションで学習した単語を使って、会話をしましょう。

ex. A: Can I have some tomato juice, please?
　　B: Alright, here you go.
　　　 Sorry, but we don't have any tomato juice.

| I will have some / a cup of / a can of / etc…, please. |
| Could I have some / a cup of / a can of / etc…, please? |
| Give me some / a cup of / a can of / etc…, please. |

## Quiz

Unit 1 で学習した単語を使って文章を完成させましょう。

| guess　sound　experience　shave　care for |

(1) Would you (　　　) another drink?
(2) Can you (　　　) what I'm thinking now?
(3) How does Sushi (　　　) for dinner?
(4) Don't you think you need to (　　　) your beard for the interview tomorrow?
(5) Do you want to (　　　) a home-stay in Australia?

| perfect　available　pure　true　original |

(6) The concert tickets are still (　　　) at the shop.
(7) I never expected him to pitch a (　　　) game.
(8) I'm wondering what the (　　　) color of your hair is?
(9) Mary is a (　　　) genius in mathematics.
(10) It may sound crazy but what I'm saying is (　　　).

# Unit 2   Shrines and Temples of Nikko

## Warm-up

**1** Listen to the recording and choose the statement that best describes each photo.

写真の説明文を聞いて、最も適切なものを A～D から選びましょう。

(1) _____

(2) _____

## Conversation 1

Henry and Emi are visiting Tosho-gu in Nikko.

**2** Listen to Conversation 1. Which of the following animals are mentioned in the conversation?

会話 1 を聞いて、会話に出てくる動物には○、出てこない動物には×をつけましょう。

(1) _____

(2) _____

(3) _____

(4) _____

(5) _____

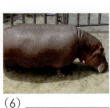

(6) _____

(7) _____

(8) _____

(9) _____

**3** Listen to Conversation 1 again. What is mentioned about each animal? Write the appropriate information on the line.

会話1をもう一度聞いて、写真の動物についてどのようなことが言われているかを考えましょう。下線部に適切な語句を書きましょう。

_____ symbolizes " _____ ."

_____ are the _____ for _____ .

_____ symbolizes " _____ "

_____ doesn't look like the real one because _____
_____ .

## Background information

**4** Listen to the background information. Choose the correct numbers or phrases.

音声を聞いて、（　　）の中の正しい語句に○をつけましょう。　　注：pilgrimage… 巡礼地

(1) Before it became the home of Tosho-gu in the (1800's / 1600's), Nikko was a pilgrimage center.
(2) The mountains surrounding Nikko have a lot of (hot springs and wildlife / hot lakes and water life).
(3) Nikko and surrounding areas are a popular sightseeing place for (either / both) international and Japanese tourists.
(4) Tosho-gu and other shrines and temples of Nikko were added to UNESCO's World Heritage list in (1990 / 1999).

Unit 2  Shrines and Temples of Nikko

## Conversation 2

Emi explains some of the history of Tosho-gu to Henry.

**5** Listen to Conversation 2. Fill in the gap with the appropriate information.

会話2を聞いて、下線部に適切な語句を書きましょう。

①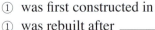

②

① was originally built by _____ for _____.

① was expanded by _____.
① was first constructed in  _____.
① was rebuilt after _____.

② is still not _____ because one of the pillars has decorations in _____ directions.

**6** Listen to Conversation 2 again. Answer the questions.

会話2をもう一度聞いて、質問に英語で答えましょう。

(1) How did Henry feel when he first saw Yomei-mon?
(2) When Tosho-gu was being built, what did the people believe about something perfect?

## Vocabulary

### Adjectives for admiration

**Learn adjectives for admiration.**　感嘆を表す形容詞を学習しましょう。

| awesome | amazing | beautiful | brilliant | fantastic | great |
| magnificent | outstanding | splendid | terrific | wonderful | |

### Words used for telling the order or time

**Learn words used for telling the order or time.**　時や順番に関係する語句を学習しましょう。

| in the 1600's | in 1999 | originally | today | later | then |
| after | before | first | second | last | |

## Useful Expressions

### Exclaiming admiration

**Practice expressions for exclaiming admiration.**　感嘆を表す表現を練習しましょう。

**Think of three places or shops that you think are great. Start a conversation about them using the vocabulary you learned in the previous section.**

あなたが素晴らしいと思う場所、店などを3つ思い浮かべましょう。Vocabulary セクションで学習した単語を使って、それについて会話をしましょう。

ex. A: The landscape here is so beautiful.
   B: Yes, indeed. It is famous for its beauty.
      Well, it is not bad, but I think … is better.
   A: I think ABC Ramen restaurant is terrific.
   B: It sure is. It is famous for its Miso-ramen.
      It's OK, but XYZ Noodle is also great.

> Wow, this/it is …
> This/It is so …
> What a … (landscape)!

## Telling the time and order

時や順番を表す表現を練習しましょう。

Research the history of your school and the biography of your favorite singer or actor/actress. Using the vocabulary and useful expressions you learned in the previous section, talk to your partner about them.

あなたの学校の沿革、好きな歌手・俳優などのバイオグラフィーを調べましょう。Vocabulary セクションで学習した単語を使って、時系列に沿ってそれをパートナーに説明しましょう。

## Quiz

Unit 2 で学習した単語を使って文章を完成させましょう。

> landscape   guardians   evil   product   imagination

(1) As (　　　), parents are expected to protect and support their children.
(2) A 15-year-old boy is old enough to know good from (　　　).
(3) Coffee is the main export (　　　) of Brazil.
(4) Children can have fun anywhere and anytime by using their (　　　).
(5) As a photographer, I have taken many (　　　) pictures over the years.

> decline   mean   carve   expand   represent

(6) Sorry, I didn't (　　　) to cause you any trouble.
(7) I'm learning how to (　　　) animals in wood.
(8) Someday I want to (　　　) my country at the Olympics.
(9) As a company owner, I'd like to (　　　) my business overseas.
(10) I didn't expect the popularity of the song would (　　　) so sharply.

# Unit 3  Ogasawara Islands

## Warm-up

**1** Listen to the recording and choose the statement that best describes each photo.

写真の説明文を聞いて、最も適切なものを A 〜 D から選びましょう。

(1) _____

(2) _____

## Conversation 1

Henry and Emi are planning their trip to Ogaswara National Park.

**2** Listen to Conversation 1. Choose the right picture that matches the conversation.

会話 1 を聞いて、内容に合う絵を選び (　　　) にその記号を書きましょう。

(1) The distance between Ogasawara Islands and Tokyo is (　　　).

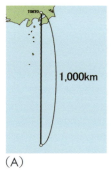
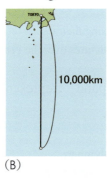

(2) Ogasawara Islands belong to (　　　).

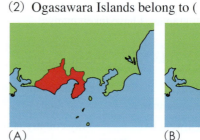

(A)　　　　　　　(B)　　　　　　　　　　　(A)　　　　　　　(B)

(3) You can get to Ogasawara Islands by (　　　).

(4) Henry suggested (　　　).

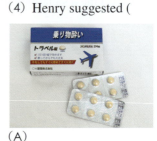

(A)　　　　　　　(B)　　　　　　　　　　　(A)　　　　　　　(B)

(5) Emi will see a (    ).  (6) Henry will go to the (    ).

(A)          (B)                (A)              (B)

**3** Listen to Conversation 1 again. Answer the questions.

会話1をもう一度聞いて、質問に英語で答えましょう。

(1) Why was a faster boat to Ogasawara Islands not put into service?
(2) What did Emi say about the medicine Henry suggested she take?

## Background information

**4** Listen to the background information. What does each number indicate? Fill in the chart with the appropriate information.

音声を聞いて、表の数字がそれぞれ何を表しているのか書きましょう。

| Number | What does it indicate? |
|--------|------------------------|
| 2011   |                        |
| 30     |                        |
| 2      |                        |
| 500    |                        |
| 43     |                        |

**5** Listen to the background information again. Answer the questions.

音声をもう一度聞いて、質問に英語で答えましょう。

(1) What is the English name for the Ogasawara Islands?
(2) What is Ogasawara sometimes referred to as?

# Unit 3  Ogasawara Islands

## Conversation 2

Henry and Emi are talking about Iwo-to on the boat to Ogasawara.

**6** Listen to Conversation 2. Fill in the blanks with the appropriate words. Look at the pictures for hints.

会話2を聞いて、ヒントの写真を見ながら（　）に適切な語句を書きましょう。

In the battle of Iwo Jima, more than 6,000 American and 20,000 Japanese soldiers (　　　　) and more than 22,000 American soldiers were (　　　　).

In the end, America (　　　) Japan.
Many (　　　) such as tanks, ships, (　　　), and aircrafts are still there deserted on Iwo-to.

The (　　　) from both sides of the battle met and (　　　) a memorial service together.

The monument reads, "Reunion of Honor"
On the 40th anniversary for the battle of Iwo Jima, American and Japanese veterans met again on these same sands. This time, in peace and friendship. We commemorate our comrades living and dead, who fought here with bravery and honor. And we pray together that our sacrifices on Iwo Jima will always be remembered and never be repeated. February 19, 1985

**7** Listen to Conversation 2 again. Answer the questions.

音声をもう一度聞いて、質問に英語で答えましょう。

(1) How long did the battle of Iwo Jima last?
(2) What are ordinary people not allowed to do?

## Vocabulary

### Words related to physical conditions

Learn words related to physical conditions. Research home remedies for these symptoms and learn more vocabulary to explain them.

病気に関係する語句を学習しましょう。これらの症状への民間療法にはどのようなものがあるか調べ、それを英語で説明する際に必要な単語も調べましょう。

| backache | headache | stomachache | toothache | cold | cough |
| fever | flu | itchy eyes | motion sickness | runny nose | seasick |
| sneeze | sore throat | medicine | tablets | pills | dentist |

## Useful Expressions

### Giving advice

Practice expressions for giving advice. Start a conversation using the vocabulary you learned in the previous section.

アドバイスをする際の表現を練習しましょう。Vocabulary セクションで学習した事柄を使って、会話をしましょう。

ex. A: I easily get seasick.
　　B: Why don't you buy some motion sickness medicine?
　　A: Sometimes that kind of medicine doesn't work at all on me.
　　B: Then, you should consult a doctor.

> Why don't you …?
> You should …
> How about …. (ing)?
> You must …

### Asking the distance and time

Practice expressions for asking the distance and time. Research the distance between your station and school/home/part-time place.

距離や所要時間を尋ねる表現を練習しましょう。駅から学校／自宅／アルバイト先などまでの距離とその所要時間などを調べ、それについて会話をしましょう。

ex. A: How far is it from here to the station?
　　B: It's about 750m.
　　A: How long will it take by bicycle?
　　B: It'll take less than 5 minutes.

### Quiz

Unit 3 で学習した単語を使って文章を完成させましょう。

| cost　service　battle　weapon　survivor |
|---|

(1) The JR line to the airport is out of (　　　) due to an accident.
(2) Tokyo won the (　　　) for the 2020 Olympic host city.
(3) I'm worried about being the only (　　　) after a big earthquake.
(4) People are not allowed to carry a (　　　) outside of their homes.
(5) The (　　　) of the bus tour to the national park is $70 per person.

| get hurt　give up　go ahead　ignore　allow |
|---|

(6) If you (　　　) someone, you pay no attention to him or her.
(7) If you fall down the stairs, you may (　　　).
(8) If you (　　　) smoking, you will decrease your chance of cancer.
(9) If you (　　　) me to change my clothes, I could join you for dinner.
(10) If you want to be rich, (　　　) and start your own business.

# Unit 4  Historic Villages of Shirakawa-go and Gokayama

## Warm-up

**1** Listen to the recording and choose the statement that best describes each photo.

写真の説明文を聞いて、最も適切なものを A〜D から選びましょう。

  (1) _____

  (2) _____

## Conversation 1

Henry and Emi are looking at a group of houses in Gokayama in Toyama Prefecture.

**2** Listen to Conversation 1. Fill in the boxes with the correct word or phrase from below.

会話 1 を聞いて、(A)〜(G) に当てはまる単語を選択肢から選んで書きましょう。

wall    angle    pillar    attic    two stories high    three stories high    roof

## 3 Listen to Conversation 1 again. Answer the questions.

会話1をもう一度聞いて、質問に英語で答えましょう。

(1) How steep is the roof of gassho-zukuri houses?
(2) What was the attic in a gassho-zukuri house used for?

# Background information

## 4 Listen to the background information. Choose the correct number or phrase.

音声を聞いて、(　　)の語句の正しい方に○をつけましょう。

| Circle the correct one | Incident |
|---|---|
| (1995 or 1990) | When gassho-zukuri houses were listed as a World Heritage site |
| (2 or 3) | The depth of the snowfall in winter in Shirakawa-go and Gokayama |
| More than (8,000 or 1,800) | The number of gassho-zukuri houses at the end of the 19th century |
| (early or middle) 20th century | When the number of gassho-zukuri houses declined |
| (1950's or 1960's) | When people started to conserve gassho-zukuri houses |
| (1,500,000 or 15,000,000) | The number of tourists who visit Shirakawa-go and Gokayama |
| (3000 or 30000) | The number of people who live in Shirakawa-go and Gokayama |

# Conversation 2

Henry and Emi are looking at the houses again in Gokayama.

## 5 Listen to Conversation 2. Number each sentence according to its order in conversation. The first one is given as an example.

会話2を聞いて、(A)～(F)の話題をヘンリーとエミが話している順番にしたがって番号をつけましょう。なお、最初の話題は (B) です。　注：re-thatch…屋根を張り替える、葺き替える

(A) The way they re-thatch the roof in recent years　　　(　　)
(B) The roof material of gassho-zukuri houses　　　　　　(　1　)
(C) The cost of re-thatching a gassho-zukuri house　　　(　　)
(D) The number of people needed for re-thatching　　　(　　)
(E) The length of durability of the roof of a gassho-zukuri house　(　　)
(F) The groups that re-thatched the roof in the past　　(　　)

# Unit 4 Historic Villages of Shirakawa-go and Gokayama

**6** Listen to Conversation 2 again. Answer the questions by filling in the missing parts.

会話2をもう一度聞いて、(1)～(5)の質問の答えを書きましょう。

(1) What is the roof material of gassho-zukuri houses called?
　　It is _____.

(2) If they re-thatched the roof of a gassho-zukuri house in a day or two, how many people would be needed?
　　_____ would be needed.

(3) If you hired people to re-thatch the roof, how much would you have to pay?
　　_____.

(4) Why are "yui" decreasing?
　　_____.

(5) Who is re-thatching gassho-zukuri houses in Gokayama now?
　　_____.

## Vocabulary

### Words for describing buildings

Learn words for describing buildings.

建物に関係する単語を学習しましょう。

| | | | |
|---|---|---|---|
| attic | backyard　basement | ceiling　entrance | floor　roof |
| staircase | steps　　　pillar | two stories high | three stories high |
| wall | a wooden building | a high-rise building | condominium studio |
| rest room | dining room | garage | living room |

## Useful Expressions

### If ... (conditional)

Practice conditional expressions.

仮定の表現を練習しましょう。

Write your ideal home using the vocabulary you learned in the previous section. Describe it to your partner using conditional expressions.

セクションで学習した単語を使って、あなたの理想の住まいを思い浮かべましょう。その家について、仮定の表現を使ってパートナーに説明しましょう。

　ex. A: If the house had a high ceiling, it would be ideal.
　　　 B: If I lived in a studio by myself, I would be happy.

Think of three situations that you wish could happen but probably would not. Using conditional expressions, talk about what you would do in those situations.

望んでいるけど実現しないこと、できたらいいと思うことを3つ思い浮かべましょう。それについて、仮定の表現を使ってパートナーに説明しましょう。

ex. A: If I had a lot of money, I could travel around the world.
　　B: If you gave me a hand, I would be able to finish the work in an hour.

> If 主語＋動詞の過去形 …, 主語＋ would/could/should 動詞 …
> If they did it in a day or two, more than 100 people would be needed.
> If you hired the people, it could cost more than 30 million yen.

## Quiz

Unit 4 で学習した単語を使って文章を完成させましょう。

　　　　　　　　pillar　roof　structure　attic　material

(1) The (　　　) of Tokyo Skytree is different from that of other tall towers.
(2) You should be careful when climbing down from the (　　　).
(3) Stone was the main building (　　　) of the pyramids of Egypt.
(4) I cannot stand staying in the (　　　) during the summer.
(5) The concrete (　　　) protects the building from a big earthquake.

　　　　　　　　complete　construct　preserve　hire　maintain

(6) We hope large companies will (　　　) more new college graduates next year.
(7) The residents are expecting the city government will (　　　) a new hospital.
(8) You should get daily exercise to (　　　) your health.
(9) It is likely to take another year to (　　　) the highway building project.
(10) People living in a foreign country cannot easily (　　　) their native culture.

# Unit 5  Historic Monuments of Ancient Kyoto

## Warm-up

**1** Listen to the recording and choose the statement that best describes each photo.

写真の説明文を聞いて、最も適切なものを A 〜 D から選びましょう。

 (1) _____

 (2) _____

## Conversation 1

Henry and Emi are window shopping in Kawaramachi area in Kyoto.

**2** Listen to Conversation 1. What items are recommended for souvenirs? Write the name of the item under each picture. Then give the reasons why they are suitable or not.

会話 1 を聞いて、A 欄の物の名前を写真の横の（　）に書きましょう。それから、それがお土産に適している場合は○を、適していない場合は×を B 欄に書きましょう。また、C 欄にその理由を書きましょう。

| A: Item | B: ○ or × | C: Reasons |
|---|---|---|
| (　　　) | | |
| (　　　) | | |
| (　　　) | | |
| (　　　) | | |
| (　　　) | | |

**3** Listen to Conversation 1 again. Answer the questions.

会話 1 をもう一度聞いて、質問に英語で答えましょう。

(1) Where does Henry's niece live and how old is she?
(2) What does Henry's niece collect?

## Background information

**4** Listen to the background information. What do these numbers indicate? Write the letter of the picture that is related to each number. You may choose the same picture more than once.

音声を聞いて、関係のある写真を選んでB欄にその記号を書きましょう。同じ写真を複数回使う場合もあります。

| A: Numbers | B: Related picture | C: What does the number indicate? |
|---|---|---|
| 794 | | |
| More than 2400 | | |
| 17 | (B) | |
| 1 | | a temple in Shiga Prefecture |
| 3 | | |
| 13 | | |
| 1 | | |
| 57 | | |
| 15 | | |

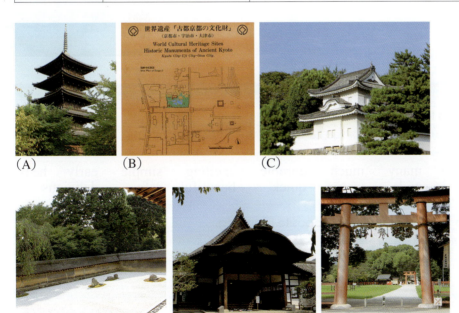

(A)　　　(B)　　　(C)

(D)　　　(E)　　　(F)

**5** Listen to the background information again. Write down what each number indicates.

音声をもう一度聞いて、各数字が何を表しているか表のC欄に書きましょう。

Unit 5　Historic Monuments of Ancient Kyoto

## Conversation 2

Henry and Emi are visiting Kozanji Temple, one of the temples listed as a UNESCO World Heritage site.

**6** Listen to Conversation 2. What is the history of tea culture in Japan? Put the sentences in their correct order. The first one is given as an example.

会話 2 を聞いて、日本の茶の文化が発展してきた順に (A) 〜 (F) の文章に番号をつけましょう。なお 1 番目は (A) です。
　　　　注：Eisai… 栄西、平安時代末期から鎌倉時代初期の僧。Myoue… 明恵、鎌倉時代初期の僧。

（A）　Eisai went to Sung and returned with tea seeds.　　　　　　　　　　　　（ 1 ）
（B）　The habit of drinking tea became popular among monks.　　　　　　　（　 ）
（C）　With the influence of Zen Buddhism, drinking tea gradually became a ceremony.　（　 ）
（D）　Myoue planted the tea seeds in Kozanji Temple.　　　　　　　　　　　（　 ）
（E）　Eisai gave tea seeds to Myoue, the founder of Kozanji Temple.　　　　（　 ）
（F）　Samurai also started drinking tea.　　　　　　　　　　　　　　　　　（　 ）

**7** Listen to Conversation 2 again. Answer the questions.

会話 2 をもう一度聞いて質問に英語で答えましょう。

（1）　How are the histories of tea and coffee similar?
（2）　Is Henry going to take a lesson in tea ceremony?

## Vocabulary

### Words for describing things

**Learn words for describing things.**

人や物事の性質や状態を表す単語を学習しましょう。

| expensive | many | much  | durable | exciting  | simple | early     | heavy |
| clean     | wide | warm  | quick   | beautiful | safe   | delicious |       |

**Learn the words that have the opposite meaning.**

上記の単語の反対の意味を持つ単語を調べましょう。

## Useful Expressions

### Refusal

**Practice expressions of refusal.**

断る際の表現を練習しましょう。

Think of gifts, books, movie/TV dramas, foods, clothes, sports or places to go that you would like to recommend. Recommend them to your partner. Your partner will refuse and give their reasons. Use the words you learned in the previous section.

あなたが人に勧めたいプレゼント、本、映画・TV ドラマ、食物、衣服、スポーツ、外出先などを思い浮かべましょう。パートナーにそれを勧めましょう。勧められた人はそれを断りましょう。Vocabulary セクションで学習した単語を使って理由をつけましょう。

ex. A: How about the Kimono we just saw in the window for your sister?
　　B: I know it's beautiful, but it's too expensive.

　　A: Why don't you read Harry Potter in English?
　　B: Thank you for your suggestion, but the story seems very complicated.

　　A: Let's try bungee jumping.
　　B: No, thanks. It's too scary.

| Suggestions | Refusal |
|---|---|
| How about…? | I'll have to decline. ( 理由 ) |
| Why don't you…? | Thanks for the offer, but ( 理由 ) |
| Let's ….. | No offense, but ( 理由 ) |
| You should…. | Actually, ( 言いにくい事 ) |
| 〈See Unit 3〉 | No, thanks. ( 理由 ) |

formal ↕ casual

## Quiz

Unit 5 で学習した単語を使って文章を完成させましょう。

　　fragile　　gorgeous　　political　　traditional　　awake

(1) More young people seem to hate the idea of having a (　　　) family.
(2) I cannot keep myself (　　　) without a cup of strong coffee.
(3) The rock band is popular for its songs with strong (　　　) messages.
(4) This is my first time to stay in such a (　　　) hotel.
(5) You need to handle this package with care because it is (　　　).

　　agony　　delivery　　ceremony　　brochure　　habit

(6) The graduation (　　　) will be held at TCU Hall on March 7.
(7) No one can avoid the (　　　) of defeat in sports.
(8) I don't know why she cannot stop her (　　　) of eating late at night.
(9) This (　　　) will help with your stay in Hawaii during the vacation.
(10) You will need to pay more if you send this package by express (　　　).

# Unit 6  Historic Monuments of Ancient Nara

## Warm-up

**1** Listen to the recording and choose the statement that best describes each photo.

写真の説明文を聞いて、最も適切なものを A ～ D から選びましょう。

(1) _____

(2) _____

## Conversation 1

Henry and Emi are now in Nara visiting the remains of Heijo-kyo, which was restored recently.

**2** Listen to Conversation 1. Which of these pictures are mentioned in the conversation? Choose the correct one.

会話 1 を聞いて、(1)～(5)の(A)と(B)のうち会話に出てくる方に○をつけましょう。

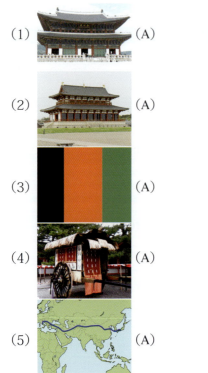
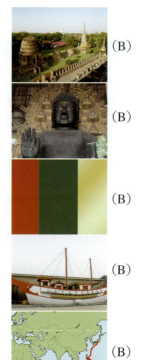

(1) (A)   (B)
(2) (A)   (B)
(3) (A)   (B)
(4) (A)   (B)
(5) (A)   (B)

### 3 Listen to Conversation 1 again. Answer the questions.

会話 1 をもう一度聞いて、質問に英語で答えましょう。

(1) Why is Henry amazed when he sees the Palace?
(2) Where were "kentoshi" sent to?
(3) Where was Nara connected to?

## Background information

### 4 Listen to the background information. Circle the correct choice.

音声を聞いて、（　）の語句のうち正しい方に○をつけましょう。

(1) Nara was the capital of Japan from (715 to 749 / 710 to 794).
(2) The (political and cultural / ethical and financial) foundation of Japan was made during the Nara period.
(3) The country which had the biggest influence on Japan was (China / Persia).
(4) Shinto shrines were built to (preserve / protect) the country.
(5) Todaiji Temple, which has (the Great Buddha / the Great Buddhist), was built during the Nara Period.
(6) Nara became a World Heritage Site in (1989 / 1998).

## Conversation 2

Henry and Emi are walking down the street in Nara and discussing the life of the ancient Japanese people.

### 5 Listen to Conversation 2. Which of the items are mentioned in the conversation?

会話 2 を聞いて、会話に出てくる物には○、出てこない物には×をつけましょう。

(1) _____ (2) _____ (3) _____ (4) _____ (5) _____

(6) _____ (7) _____ (8) _____ (9) _____

*31*

## 6 Listen to Conversation 2 again. Answer the questions.

会話2をもう一度聞いて、質問に英語で答えましょう。

(1) What furniture did the emperor and government officials use?
(2) What did they use the furniture for?

## Vocabulary

### Household objects

**Learn the names of the things in your house.**

家の中にある物の名前を学習しましょう。

| mat | rug | carpet | shelf | chest of drawers |
| cabinet | sofa/couch | ottoman | coffee table | armchair |
| bookcase | table lamp | floor lamp | cupboard | |

この他に家の中にある家具などを思い浮かべ、その英訳を調べましょう。

### Words for expressing astonishment

**Learn the words for expressing astonishment.**

驚きを表す単語を学習しましょう。

| amazed | amazing | surprised | surprising | astonished | astonishing |
| awesome | brilliant | incredible | unbelievable | marvelous | shocked |
| shocking | terrific | | | | |

## Useful Expressions

### Expressing astonishment

**Practice expressions for astonishment.**

驚きを表す表現を練習しましょう。

**You are at your friend's home. S/he has good quality or convenient furniture. Express your astonishment using the words you learned in the previous section.**

友達の家に遊びに行きました。部屋には上質の家具、便利な家具がたくさんあってあなたは驚いています。Vocabulary セクションで学習した語句を使って、それを伝えましょう。

ex. A: Wow, it's amazing. This sofa is really comfortable!
    B: Yeah. I could sleep on it forever.

    A: Oh, my goodness. I'm surprised at the number of books your bookcase can hold.
    B: Yes, it's very convenient.

> That's/It's awesome/amazing/surprising/crazy …
> I'm astonished that …
> Wow!
> Oh, my goodness!  Oh, my god!

## Quiz

Unit 6 で学習した単語を使って文章を完成させましょう。

| remind   cross   lead   connect   wonder |
|---|

(1) Your positive thinking and attitude can (　　　) to success in life.
(2) It's dangerous for schoolchildren to (　　　) the busy street.
(3) These photos (　　　) me of my happy high school days.
(4) SNS can (　　　) us quickly to anyone around the world.
(5) I (　　　) how she's perfectly mastered three foreign languages.

| combination   reveal   terminal   fail   atmosphere |
|---|

(6) I don't believe Tom would (　　　) our secret.
(7) I'm afraid Chris might (　　　) to arrive in time for the appointment.
(8) We'd like to dine at a restaurant that has a quiet and romantic (　　　).
(9) Milk tea and tuna onigiri make the worst breakfast (　　　).
(10) Tokyo Station is a (　　　) for the Tokaido Shinkansen.

# Unit 7  Sacred Sites and Pilgrims Routes in the Kii Mountain Range

## Warm-up

**1** Listen to the recording and choose the statement that best describes each photo.

写真の説明文を聞いて、最も適切なものをA～Dから選びましょう。

(1) _____

(2) _____

## Conversation 1

Henry and Emi are walking on the path of Kumano Kodo.

**2** Listen to Conversation 1. Fill in the chart about visiting Kumano with the appropriate information.

会話1を聞いて、熊野詣を説明する下の表の(A)～(G)を埋めましょう。 注：ascetic practices… 苦行

| When? | Who? | How many times? |
|---|---|---|
| Originally | (A) | |
| Heian period | (B) | 1 ＋ 9 times |
| | (C) | (E) |
| | ex-emperor Toba | (F) |
| | (D) | 28 times |
| Later | common people | (G) |

**3** Listen to Conversation 1 again. Answer the questions.

会話1をもう一度聞いて、質問に英語で答えましょう。

(1) The path Henry and Emi are walking on was popular among travelers. Where did the travelers come from?

(2) Besides religious reasons, why did ex-emperors visit Kumano so often?

## Background information

**4** Listen to the background information. Circle the correct choice.

音声を聞いて、(　　) の語句の正しい方に○をつけましょう。

(1) Some of the Kumano area was listed on the UNESCO World Heritage Site in ( 2004 / 2011 ).
(2) The area covers ( 494.3 / 495.3 ) hectares.
(3) The area is the ( newest / biggest ) Cultural Heritage site in Japan.
(4) The area is famous for its heavy ( rainfalls / rainbows ).
(5) In 2011 the area was heavily damaged by ( a typhoon / a slide door ).
(6) ( 50 / 15 ) meters of the Kumano Kodo was buried under mud.
(7) The rocks in the waterfall's ( basic / basin ) were carried away by a large amount of ( mud / water ).

## Conversation 2

Henry and Emi are looking at a banner near a torii at Kumano Hongu Taisha.

**5** Listen to Conversation 2. Which item in the picture are they talking about? Choose from A to G.

会話 2 を聞いて、ヘンリーとエミが話題にしているものに○をつけましょう。

Unit 7  Sacred Sites and Pilgrims Routes in the Kii Mountain Range

**6** Listen to Conversation 2 again. Fill in the blanks with the appropriate information.
会話2をもう一度聞いて、空欄に適切な語句を書きましょう。

(1) _____ is a symbol of the _____ and appears in Japanese _____.

(2) _____ the emperor Jinmu and his army to Yamato.

(3) Henry might have seen _____ at the _____.

(4) Why has _____ come to be a symbol of football in Japan?

Reason 1. _____.
Reason 2. _____.
Reason 3. _____.

## Vocabulary

### Words describing feelings

Learn vocabulary describing feelings and physical conditions.
心や体の状態を表す語句を学習しましょう。

| angry   furious   upset      nervous    tense      hungry   tired   sick |
| sad     mad       depressed  irritated  disgusted  scared   embarrassed  |
| confused  disappointed  dizzy  feverish  itchy  painful  drowsy          |

Think of a daily situation where you made a mistake and describe it with the verbs below.
次の動詞を使って、日常生活で起きる小さな失敗、事件、事故を表現できます。どのようなことが言えるか、動詞の後に続く語句を考えましょう。

| miss    lose    forget    fall    drop |

ex. I missed the train. I lost my key. I forgot about the test.

# Useful Expressions

## must/might + have

**Practice expressions for past probability.**

過去のことに関する推量の表現を練習しましょう。

Situation 1: Your friend didn't talk to you at all yesterday. Guess the reason and express it with the vocabulary you learned in the previous section.

状況1：友人が昨日、まったく口をきいてくれませんでした。その理由を推測し、Vocabulary セクションで学習した語句を使って表現しましょう。

ex. A: Takashi didn't talk to us at all yesterday, did he?
    B: No, he didn't. He must have …

Situation 2: Your friend didn't come to see you at the appointed place. Guess the reason and express it with the vocabulary you learned in the previous section.

状況2：友人が昨日、約束の場所に来ませんでした。その理由を推測し、Vocabulary セクションで学習した語句を使って表現しましょう。

ex. A: Kaori didn't come to see us yesterday.
    B: No, she didn't. She must have …

## Quiz

Unit 7 で学習した単語を使って文章を完成させましょう。

| conquer | nobles | frequent | emperors | sacred |
|---|---|---|---|---|

(1) (          ) in Europe needed great military power to control all their people and territory.
(2) Powerful nations used to (          ) other nations for economic and religious dominance.
(3) (          ) are people who belong to a high social class and have titles.
(4) The sword, jewel and mirror were (          ) treasures of the Japanese emperors.
(5) Young workers cannot create stable lives because of (          ) job changes.

| monks | lay people | show off | suffer | common |
|---|---|---|---|---|

(6) I hate seeing Hollywood movie stars (          ) their gorgeous life.
(7) (          ) live a simple life, focusing the mind on spiritual matters.
(8) Extreme hot weather is becoming more (          ) around the world.
(9) Religious people view the world differently from (          ).
(10) My mother used to (          ) from painful headaches for over ten years.

# Unit 8  Himeji-jo

## Warm-up

**1** Listen to the recording and choose the statement that best describes each photo.

写真の説明文を聞いて、最も適切なものを A 〜 D から選びましょう。

 (1) _____      (2) _____

## Conversation 1

Henry and Emi are touring Himeji Castle in Hyogo Prefecture.

**2** Listen to Conversation 1. Fill in the chart with the appropriate information.

会話 1 を聞いて、日本の江戸時代の人々の職業名 ( 社会階層 ) とそれぞれがどのような事柄を求められていたかについて表の (1) 〜 (8) を埋めましょう。

| What were they called? | What were they supposed to do to contribute the society? |
|---|---|
| (1) | (2) |
| farmers | (3) |
| (4) | (5) |
| (6) | (7) |
| daimyo families | (8) What were they required to do? |

**3** Listen to Conversation 1 again. Answer the questions.

会話1をもう一度聞いて、質問に英語で答えましょう。

(1) When did Japanese society become rigid?
(2) What did daimyo have to do every other year?

## Background information

**4** Listen to the background information and decide if each statement is true or false. Write T for true and F for false, underline and correct the false words or phrases.

音声を聞いて、(1)〜(7)が内容と合っていればT、合っていなければFを(　)に書きましょう。Fの文章の間違いに下線を引いて音声の内容に合うように書き直しましょう。

(1) Himeji Castle was Japan's first UNESCO World Heritage Site.　(　)
(2) Himeji Castle is the second largest and most popular Japanese castle.　(　)
(3) Himeji Castle wasn't destroyed during the bombing of Himeji City.　(　)
(4) Himeji Castle was severely damaged by the Great Hanshin Earthquake.　(　)
(5) Himeji Castle was first built in 1346.　(　)
(6) Himeji Castle was given to Tokugawa Ieyasu after the Battle of Sekigahara.　(　)
(7) The present castle was built by Toyotomi Hideyoshi.　(　)

## Conversation 2

Henry notices a rack of weapons when Henry and Emi are exploring Himeji Castle and starts explaining how to make katana.

**5** Listen to Conversation 2. Fill in the chart with appropriate information.

会話2を聞いて、日本刀の制作過程について表の(1)〜(4)に適切な写真を(A)〜(D)から選びましょう。それから(5)〜(9)に適切な語句を書きましょう。

| Photo | Explanation | |
|---|---|---|
| | The smith makes the two blocks of steel from some pieces of preselected steel. | |
| | The smith (5 _____ ) the steel 10 to 13 times. | |
| (1) _____ | The smith (6 _____ | ) the steel into the basic shape of the sword. |
| (2) _____ | The smith (7 _____ | ) some wet clay to the sword. |
| (3) _____ | The smith (8 _____ | ) the metal again. |
| (4) _____ | The smith (9 _____ | ) the whole sword into water. |

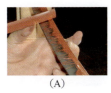　　　

　　(A)　　　　　　　　(B)　　　　　　　　(C)　　　　　　　　(D)

Unit 8  Himeji-jo

**6** Listen to Conversation 2 again. Answer the questions.
会話 2 をもう一度聞いて、質問に英語で答えましょう。

(1) How much does a Japanese sword cost?
(2) Why are katana expensive?

## Vocabulary

### Words for describing occupations

Learn words for describing occupations.
職業に関係する語句を学習しましょう。

| farmer | craftsman | merchant | fisherman | architect | fire fighter |
| civil servant | police officer | computer programmer | sales person | engineer |
| writer | designer | nurse | technical expert | teacher | researcher |

Think of other occupations and learn the English words for them.
他にどのような職業があるかを考え、その英語名称を調べましょう。

## Useful Expressions

### Obligation/Need

Practice expressions of obligation and need.
義務や必要の表現を練習しましょう。

What are the people of the occupations you learned in the previous section supposed to do? Talk about it with your partner.
Vocabulary セクションで学習した職業の人は何をすることを求められていますか。パートナーと話し合いましょう。

ex. A: What are police officers supposed to do?
　　B: They are always supposed to help people in trouble.

　　A: What is expected of architects?
　　B: They are expected to design a good house.

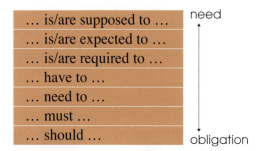

## Quiz

Unit 8 で学習した単語を使って文を完成させましょう。

| authentic productive complicated basic severe |
|---|

(1) Free speech should be considered a (　　　) human right.
(2) Nobody seemed to be interested in his long (　　　) story.
(3) Many experts do not recommend using (　　　) punishments to teach your children self-control.
(4) Morning people are healthier, happier, and more (　　　) than evening people.
(5) Restaurant Mikado is very popular because it serves (　　　) Japanese food.

| enforce summarize fold dip contribute |
|---|

(6) My kids found it difficult to (　　　) their clothes properly.
(7) The instructor advised me to (　　　) the main points of my speech.
(8) When eating sushi, you should (　　　) only the fish side of the nigiri into soy sauce.
(9) Eating a balanced diet and taking regular exercise (　　　) to good health.
(10) The government must (　　　) the new employment law carefully.

# Unit 9  Hiroshima Genbaku Dome

## Warm-up

**1** Listen to the recording and choose the statement that best describes each photo.

写真の説明文を聞いて、最も適切なものを A 〜 D から選びましょう。

(1) _____

(2) _____

## Conversation 1

Emi and Henry are visiting the Atomic-Bomb Dome.

**2** Listen to Conversation 1. Who said the following words or phrases? Write H for Henry and E for Emi.

会話 1 を聞いて、誰が次の語句を言っているのかを考えましょう。ヘンリーが言っていれば H、エミが言っていれば E を (　) に書きましょう。

(1) Atomic-Bomb Dome　　　　　　　　　(　)
(2) history textbook　　　　　　　　　　 (　)
(3) speechless　　　　　　　　　　　　　(　)
(4) A-bomb　　　　　　　　　　　　　　(　)
(5) fall apart　　　　　　　　　　　　　 (　)
(6) will power　　　　　　　　　　　　　(　)
(7) a symbol of perseverance and peace　　(　)
(8) must-see　　　　　　　　　　　　　　(　)

**3** Listen to Conversation 1 again. Answer the questions.

会話 1 をもう一度聞いて、質問に英語で答えましょう。

(1) Where has Henry seen the Atomic-Bomb Dome before?
(2) How long has the Atomic-Bomb Dome been standing?
(3) What are two things the Dome symbolizes?

## Background information

**4** Listen to the background information. Each sentence below includes incorrect information. Correct it with the right information.

音声を聞いて (1) ～ (7) の文章の間違いを探して下線を引き、( ) に正しい語句を書きましょう。

(1) The first atomic bomb used as a weapon exploded on August 5 in 1945.　　(　　　)
(2) The atomic bomb had the codename Little Baby.　　(　　　)
(3) The atomic bomb exploded 900 meters above Shima Surgical Clinic with the power of 12 kilotons of dynamite.　　(　　　)
(4) The fireball created by the nuclear reaction was 370 meters in diameter and reached temperatures of 3,890°C.　　(　　　)
(5) The firestorm burnt down everything within 11 hectares.　　(　　　)
(6) About 130,000 to 160,000, or 30% of Hiroshima's population, died in the first blast.　　(　　　)
(7) The Hirosima Peace Memorial also expresses the hope for world peace and the ultimate destination of all nuclear weapons.　　(　　　)

## Conversation 2

Emi and Henry visit the Peace Museum for the first time.

**5** Listen to Conversation 2. Circle the words below that are used in the conversation. Classify the circled words as either a noun or adjective.

会話 2 を聞いて、出てきた単語に〇をつけましょう。〇をつけた単語を名詞と形容詞に分類しましょう。

| awful | thrilling | moving | pain | horrified | heartbreaking |
| shocked | suffering | peaceful | sleepy | loneliness | happy |
| bored | little | saddened | horror | angry | |

| noun | |
|---|---|
| adjective | |

Unit 9   Hiroshima Genbaku Dome

**6** Listen to Conversation 2 again. Fill in the blanks with the appropriate information.

会話2をもう一度聞いて、（　）に適切な語句を書きましょう。

(1) Emi felt (　　　　) when she saw the picture (　　).
(2) Henry felt (　　　　) when he saw the picture (　　).
(3) The visitors in the museum felt (　　　　) when they saw the picture (A).

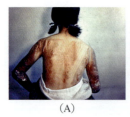
(A)

(B)

(C)

写真提供：広島平和記念資料館（撮影者・作者：川原四儀、小松キクエ）

## Vocabulary

### Units of measurement

Learn vocabulary for units of measurement.
数字に関係する語句を学習しましょう。

| | | | | | |
|---|---|---|---|---|---|
| 5cm | 5m | 5km | 25cm² | 125m³ | 50kmh |
| 20°C | 3g | 3kg | 3t | 5in | 5ft |
| 5yd | 5mi | 5mph | 68°F | 5oz | 5lbs |

## Useful Expressions

### Expressing feelings of obligation with causative words

Practice expressing feelings of obligation with causative words.

「…（物、事）が（人）に…させる」＝「…（物、事）によって（人）が…になる」という表現を練習しましょう。

Using the words you learned in the previous page, tell your partner what makes you feel a certain feeling.

前のページで学習した形容詞と名詞を使って、あなたは何によってどのような気持ちになるかをパートナーに伝えましょう。

ex. A: What makes you angry?
　　B: Bob. Bob's careless words always make me very angry.

　　A: What makes you sleepy?
　　B: Hot milk makes me sleepy.

## Asking the distance, speed, temperature, weight, etc.

Practice expressions for asking the distance, speed, temperature, weight, etc.

距離や速さ、温度や重さなどを尋ねる表現を練習しましょう。

Research the distances between A and B, the area of a place, the speed of a plane/train, the weight of a thing, the temperature of a city. Practice asking for those measurements using the previous section's vocabulary.

ある地点から別の地点までの距離、ある場所の面積、乗り物の速度、物の重量、世界の都市の気温などを調べましょう。Vocabulary セクションで学習した語句を使って、それらを尋ねる練習をしましょう。

ex. A: How big is Tokyo Dome?
    B: It's 47,500$m^3$.

    A: What is the average temperature of Honolulu?
    B: It's about 26°C.

> How (far/high 〈形容詞〉) is …?
> What is (the highest speed 〈名詞〉 of) …?
> How much (does it weigh 〈動詞〉)…?

## Quiz

Unit 9 で学習した単語を使って文章を完成させましょう。

| speechless    incredible    aware    lasting    realize |
|---|

(1) Teenagers should be more (　　　) of the dangers online.
(2) Many studies show that bullying has (　　　) effects on the victims.
(3) It is (　　　) that the blind pianist won the first prize in the competition.
(4) His selfish behavior made me (　　　) with anger.
(5) I began to (　　　) that my brother and I live in two different worlds.

| glimpse    radiation    horror    remain    preserve |
|---|

(6) Some students (　　　) silent when their teachers ask them some questions in class.
(7) Using salt is one way to (　　　) food for a long period of time.
(8) People learned about the destructive power of an earthquake and the (　　　) of a tsunami.
(9) We should avoid being exposed to high levels of (　　　).
(10) I got a (　　　) of Mt. Fuji from the window of the airplane.

# Unit 10   Itsukushima Shinto Shrine

## Warm-up

**1** Listen to the recording and choose the statement that best describes each photo.

写真の説明文を聞いて、最も適切なものを A〜D から選びましょう。

(1) _____

(2) _____

## Conversation 1

Henry and Emi are visiting Itsukushima Shrine in Miyajima.

**2** Listen to Conversation 1. What are Henry and Emi looking at now? Put N for the things they are looking at now, and L for the things they will see later.

会話 1 を聞いて、ヘンリーとエミが今見ているものには N を、後で見るものには L を書きましょう。

(1) _____

(2) _____

(3) _____

(4) _____

(5) _____

(6) _____

(7) _____

**3** Listen to Conversation 1 again. Answer the questions.

会話1をもう一度聞いて、質問に英語で答えましょう。

(1) How big is the Miyajima Torii gate?
(2) According to legend, how did the ponds appear when the shrine was first made?
(3) How does the torii look when the tide is full?

## Background information

**4** Listen to the background information. Fill in the chart with the appropriate information.

音声を聞いて、表を適切な語句で埋めましょう。

| The year Miyajima was added to the UNESCO's list | |
|---|---|
| Miyajima is traditionally considered | |
| Reasons why the shrine was built over the water | |
| People with a serious illness and women giving birth are supposed to | |
| Other attractions of Miyajima | |

Unit 10  Itsukushima Shinto Shrine

## Conversation 2

Henry and Emi are walking around Miyajima.

**5** Listen to Conversation 2. Arrange the pictures in the order that they are mentioned. The last one is given as an example.

会話 2 を聞いて、(A) 〜 (F) の写真を会話に出てくる順番に並べましょう。なお、最後に来る写真は A です。

(A) ___6___

(B) _____

(C) _____

(D) _____

(E) _____

(F) _____

**6** Listen to Conversation 2 again. Answer the questions.

会話 2 をもう一度聞いて、質問に英語で答えましょう。

(1) How long will it take to walk up to the top of Mt. Misen?
(2) What will Henry and Emi do with the money saved from not taking the ropeway?
(3) What are Henry and Emi enjoying at the top of Mt. Misen?

## Vocabulary

### Words for describing sequence

Learn words for describing sequence.

時の前後関係を表す語句を学習しましょう。

| when | while | after | before | as soon as |
| soon after | long before | since | until | by the time |

# Useful Expressions

## Sequence

**Practice expressions for sequence.**

前後関係のあるものごとの表現を練習しましょう。

Based on your understanding of Conversation 2, fill in the blanks with the appropriate information. The words in italics are hints. Compare your answers with your partner's.

会話2のヘンリーとエミの行動について、斜字体になっている語句に注意して空欄を埋めましょう。パートナーの答えと比べてみましょう。

(1) *When* Henry and Emi _____ , they were surprised.
(2) Henry and Emi decided to walk up the mountain *after* they _____ .
(3) *While* _____ , they sweated a lot.
(4) Henry and Emi had been walking for 90 minutes *since* they _____ .
(5) *As soon as* Henry reached the top of the mountain, he _____ .
(6) Emi drank some water *before* _____ .
(7) Soon *after* Emi drank some water, she _____ .

会話2の続きを想像して空欄を埋めましょう。

(8) Henry and Emi will enjoy the beautiful scenery *until* _____ .
(9) *By the time* Henry and Emi come back to the shrine, _____ .
(10) Henry and Emi will be starving *long before* _____ .

## Quiz

Unit 10 で学習した単語を使って文章を完成させましょう。

| fare | single | tiny | spot | save |
|---|---|---|---|---|

(1) The local bus (　　　) will increase by 20 % at the end of this year.
(2) My dream is building a (　　　) house in the beautiful woods.
(3) Every (　　　) member of our group has his or her own role to play.
(4) You should learn from smart travelers about how to (　　　) time and money on travel.
(5) Hakone is a well-known and popular holiday (　　　) in Japan.

| float | gigantic | miss | brochure | legend |
|---|---|---|---|---|

(6) My mother said she would (　　　) me a lot after I left home for college.
(7) The (　　　) says that there once were man-killing beasts in the village.
(8) Some (　　　) companies are powerful enough to affect the nation's economic policy.
(9) I was surprised to see the volcanic rock (　　　) on the water surface.
(10) A colorful (　　　) with current local maps will attract tourists from overseas.

# Unit 11　Yakushima

## Warm-up

**1** Listen to the recording and choose the statement that best describes each photo.

写真の説明文を聞いて、最も適切なものを A ～ D から選びましょう。

(1) _____

(2) _____

## Conversation 1

Henry and Emi are about to hike through the sugi forest of Yakushima.

**2** Listen to Conversation 1. What items below does Henry have in his backpack? What other items does Emi have in her backpack? Put H for Henry and E for Emi.

会話 1 を聞いて、ヘンリーのリュックに入っている物に H、エミのリュックに入っている物に E を書きましょう。

(1) _____

(2) _____

(3) _____

(4) _____

(5) _____

(6) _____

(7) _____

(8) _____

(9) _____

(10) _____

**3** Listen to Conversation 1 again. Answer the questions.

会話 1 をもう一度聞いて、質問に英語で答えましょう。

(1) Where did Emi find Henry's raincoat?
(2) Why are hiking polls helpful?
(3) How can you prevent catching a cold or hurting your feet while hiking?

## Background information

**4** Listen to the background information. Each statement below has incorrect information. Underline the incorrect part and write the appropriate words or phrases in (　).

音声を聞いて、(1) 〜 (8) の文章の間違いを探して下線を引き、(　) に正しい語句を書きましょう。

(1) Yakushima became a World Heritage site in 1995.　(　　　　　　　　)
(2) Yakushima is on the southern tip of the Ryukyu island chain.　(　　　　　　　　)
(3) Jomonsugi is 16.2m tall.　(　　　　　　　　)
(4) Jomonsugi is as old as 1200 years.　(　　　　　　　　)
(5) Yakushima has less rainfall than the Japan's average.　(　　　　　　　　)
(6) About 200,000 tourists visit Yakushima every year.　(　　　　　　　　)
(7) In Yakushima, farming is a major source of income.　(　　　　　　　　)
(8) Yakushima never has snow.　(　　　　　　　　)

## Conversation 2

Henry and Emi have arrived at Jomonsugi and start to discuss tree worship around the world.

**5** Listen to Conversation 2. Fill in the chart with appropriate information.

会話 2 を聞いて、表の (1) 〜 (6) を適切な語句で埋めましょう。注：kauri tree… ナギモドキ属の樹木。アカチス、カウリ

| Jomonsugi | doesn't have (1　　　　　　　), was (2　　　　　　　) with a kauri tree in New Zealand in the program "The Family of Ancient Trees". | |
|---|---|---|
| Sacred trees of the world | Tree of knowledge | (3) ⟨ In which culture? ⟩ |
| | Banyan and Peepal trees | (4) ⟨ In which culture? ⟩ |
| | Bodhi tree | (5) ⟨ In which culture? ⟩ |
| | Christmas tree | (6) ⟨ In which culture? ⟩ |

**6** Listen to Conversation 2 again. Answer the questions.

会話 2 をもう一度聞いて質問に英語で答えましょう。

(1) What is Henry surprised about?
(2) What do trees provide us?

# Unit 11  Yakushima

## Vocabulary

### Adjectives for describing things

**Learn adjectives for describing things.**

物質の状態、味覚を表す語句を学習しましょう。

| huge | large | good | warm | dry | tasty | sweet |
|------|-------|------|------|-----|-------|-------|
| bitter | salty | spicy | tender | fatty | delicious | crispy |

**Learn synonyms and antonyms of the words above.**

上の単語の同義語と反対語を調べましょう。

### Verbs relating to our five senses

**Learn verbs related to our five senses.**

五感に関係する語句を学びましょう。

| look | sound | smell | feel | taste |

## Useful Expressions

### Comparatives and superlatives

**Practice comparative and superlative expressions.**

二つの物や人を比べたり、複数の物や人の中で「最も〜である」いう表現を練習しましょう。

**Think of the most/…est things. Using vocabulary you learned in the previous section, tell your partner about it. Your partner will answer your statement using more/…er.**

Vocabulary セクションで学習した単語を使って、最も〜である物や事柄を考え、それをパートナーに伝えましょう。パートナーは、「より〜なものがある」という返事をしましょう。

ex. A: Yakushima is the wettest place in Japan.
   B: No, I don't think so. My apartment is wetter!!!

   A: This is the most delicious curry and rice I've ever eaten.
   B: Well, actually, I can make more delicious curry and rice than this one.

| A is the 形容詞＋est/most 形容詞原形 … | (Aが一番…) |
|---|---|
| B is the second 形容詞＋est/most 形容詞原形 … | (Bが二番めに…) |
| A is 形容詞＋er / more 形容詞原形 than D | (A>D) |
| C is as 形容詞原形 as … | (C=A) |
| E is twice as 形容詞原形 as F … | (E=2×F) |

## Similarities

### Practice similarity expressions.
類似を表す表現を練習しましょう。

Using vocabulary you learned in the previous section, fill in the blanks.
Vocabulary セクションで学習した単語を使って空欄に当てはまる語句を考え、「A は B のようだ」という内容でパートナーと会話をしましょう。

```
... looks/sounds ... like 名詞・名詞句
... looks/sounds... 形容詞
```

ex. A: Jomonsugi looks like a giant.
    B: Yes, it also looks like a huge tower.

(1) My mother's voice sounds (like) _____ .
(2) A crowed train on a rainy day smells (like) _____ .
(3) This silk scarf feels (like) _____ .
(4) This cake tastes (like) _____ .
(5) Going _____ like a perfect plan.
(6) Your _____ gorgeous!

## Quiz

Unit 11 で学習した単語を使って文章を完成させましょう。

| emergency | notice | pack | shelter | ready |
|---|---|---|---|---|

(1) I still haven't gotten my room (　　　) for my guests arriving in an hour.
(2) You should take (　　　) quickly if you hear thunder or see lightning.
(3) You will need different sizes of moving boxes to (　　　) items of different sizes.
(4) In most (　　　) situations, timing could be the key to saving someone's life.
(5) I wonder why I didn't (　　　) that she needed my support while seeking a job.

| partner | fuel | extra | universal | worship |
|---|---|---|---|---|

(6) The fact is that English is still the (　　　) language of business.
(7) More major Japanese automakers will (　　　) with foreign rivals in the near future.
(8) (　　　) charges and taxes will be added to some products you imported from Europe.
(9) Young athletes of today tend to (　　　) Olympic gold medalists as their heroes.
(10) This new model car can save 20 percent more (　　　) than the previous one.

# Unit 12  Gusuku Sites and Related Properties of the Kingdom of Ryukyu

## Warm-up

**1** Listen to the recording and choose the statement that best describes each photo.

写真の説明文を聞いて、最も適切なものを A ～ D から選びましょう。

(1) _____

(2) _____

## Conversation 1

Henry and Emi are on a plane flying over Okinawa.

**2** Listen to Conversation 1. Fill in the chart of Okinawan history with the appropriate information.

会話 1 を聞いて、沖縄の歴史についての表の (1) ～ (11) に適切な語句を書きましょう。

| Years | State/condition/incident | Extra information |
|---|---|---|
| For 450 years | (1) | Influenced and controlled by Ming and (2) _____ ) and (3) _____ ). |
| 1879 | (4) | (5) |
| March-June, 1945 | (6) | (7) |
| 1945-1972 | (8) | |
| 1972 | (9) | (10) |
| Now | (11) | Over 5 million tourists visit each year. |

**3** Listen to Conversation 1 again. Answer the questions.

会話 1 をもう一度聞いて、質問に英語で答えましょう。

(1) How does Henry describe the sea of Okinawa?
(2) How many people were killed in the battle of Okinawa?
(3) What does Henry appreciate?

## Background information

**4** Write T if the statement is true and F if the statement is false.

音声を聞いて、(1)〜(7) が内容と合っていれば T、合っていなければ F を書きましょう。

(1) The Gusuku sites of the Kingdom of Ryukyu were listed as World Heritage sites in 2010.
(　　　)
(2) Gusuku means castle in the Okinawan language. (　　　)
(3) Shuri-jo was used mainly as a guest house for visitors. (　　　)
(4) Shuri-jo was restored in 1992. (　　　)
(5) Two castles out of six have been restored. (　　　)
(6) Shikina-en, which was the second house of the Ryukyu kings, was originally constructed in the 18th century. (　　　)
(7) Shikina-en was restored in 1992. (　　　)

**5** Listen to the background information again and correct the mistakes in the sentences marked with F.

音声をもう一度聞いて、Fの文章の間違いを訂正しましょう。

## Conversation 2

Henry and Emi are walking on the main street in Naha.

**6** Listen to Conversation 2. Put the sentences below in their correct order. The first one is given as an example.

会話2を聞いて、(A)〜(H) のトピックを会話に出てくる順番に並べましょう。最初のトピックは (G) です。

(A) Emi will take Henry to her favorite Okinawan restaurant. (　　　)
(B) People in Okinawa believe that food is the best medicine. (　　　)
(C) Henry feels he is lucky to have a chance to eat unusual things. (　　　)
(D) Emi said she had eaten some parts of pigs before. (　　　)
(E) Henry was surprised to know that Okinawan people eat every part of the pig. (　　　)
(F) Emi recommends Tofu made from peanuts and goya chanpuru. (　　　)
(G) Emi suggested having a party. (　1　)
(H) Okinawa is well known for longevity. (　　　)

**7** Listen to Conversation 2 again. Answer the questions.

会話2をもう一度聞いて質問に英語で答えましょう。

(1) What did Henry notice on the streets in Okinawa?
(2) According to Emi, what are the ears and hands of pigs good for?

Unit 12　Gusuku Sites and Related Properties of the Kingdom of Ryukyu

## Vocabulary

### Words for describing your personality

**Learn words for describing personality.**

人の性格に関係する語句を学習しましょう。

| | | | | | |
|---|---|---|---|---|---|
| nice | honest | attractive | friendly | charming | sincere |
| straightforward | | considerate | generous | terrific | outgoing |
| active | optimistic | passionate | sociable | reliable | responsible |
| mature | unselfish | polite | humble | tidy | energetic |

**Learn synonyms and antonyms of the words above.**

上記の語句の同義語、反意語を調べましょう。

### Verbs for cooking

**Learn verbs for cooking.**

料理に関係する語句を学習しましょう。

| | | | | | | | | |
|---|---|---|---|---|---|---|---|---|
| cook | boil | grill | bake | roast | broil | deep fry | stir fry | steam |
| simmer | heat | mix | pour | dip | squeeze | crash | roll | knead |
| baste | cut | slice | chop | peel | season | put | add | brown |

## Useful Expressions

### Commenting on someone's statement

**Practice commenting on someone's statement.**

相手が言ったことに対するあなたの感想を表す表現を練習しましょう。

**Using the words in the previous section, tell your partner about your family and a friend. Your partner will comment on it.**

Vocabularyセクションで学習した単語を使ってあなたの家族や友人などをパートナーに説明しましょう。パートナーはそれに対して感想を述べましょう。

　　ex. A:　My new boyfriend is very attractive.
　　　　B:　Great. I'm happy to hear that.
　　　　　　Oh, I'm jealous of you.

　　　　A:　My ex-husband wasn't generous at all.
　　　　B:　You're lucky that you're separated.
　　　　　　Oh, I'm sure (that) you're lying.

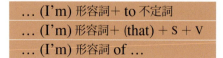

… (I'm) 形容詞 + to 不定詞
… (I'm) 形容詞 + (that) + S + V
… (I'm) 形容詞 of …

## Explaining how to do things

Practice expressions explaining how to do things.

物事の手順を説明する表現を練習しましょう。

Research your local cuisine. Tell your partner how to make it.

あなたの街の郷土料理の調理法を調べましょう。パートナーに作り方を説明しましょう。

ex. Here's how to cook goya chanpuru.
First, you slice a goya and soak it in the water.
Season the pork with salt and pepper.
Next, put some oil in a pan and brown tofu in it.
Remove the tofu and add some more oil in the pan.
Then, stir fry the goya and pork in the pan.
Put the tofu back and add some sake, soy sauce, salt and pepper.
Adding bonito flakes make it more delicious.
Finally, beat the egg and pour it over.

It tastes a bit bitter, but sure is yummy!!

## Quiz

Unit12で学習した単語を使って文章を完成させましょう。

| independent　　severe　　unusual　　peaceful　　delicious |
|---|

（1） In recent years, we have witnessed (　　　　) weather conditions.
（2） We'd like to dine at a restaurant that serves healthy and (　　　　) meals.
（3） He has been suffering from (　　　　) headaches for years.
（4） Your life is great when you have (　　　　) relationships with others.
（5） Being jobless makes it difficult for young people to be (　　　　)from their parents.

| restore　　appreciate　　prevent　　destroy　　recommend |
|---|

（6） We should take action to (　　　　) drunk driving accidents.
（7） A computer virus could (　　　　) your PC hardware and database.
（8） The earthquake victims (　　　　) all the volunteer workers have done for them.
（9） Doctors (　　　　) that people avoid eating or drinking within 2 hours before bedtime.
（10） Experts say it will take more time and effort to (　　　　) the Japanese economy.

# Epilogue

 Emi received an e-mail from Henry.

**1** Listen to the e-mail and following 6 sentences. Correct the mistakes in each sentence.

音声を聞いて、(1)〜(6) の英文の間違いを訂正しましょう。

| | | |
|---|---|---|
| × | (1) | Henry thought the trip was a waste of time. |
| ○ | | |
| × | (2) | Henry wasn't satisfied with Emi's work. |
| ○ | | |
| × | (3) | Shiretoko and Tokyo were Henry's favorite World Heritage sites. |
| ○ | | |
| × | (4) | Henry thinks that Japanese cook books focus too much on cities. |
| ○ | | |
| × | (5) | Henry liked the cities in Japan because they had a "samurai" feel to them. |
| ○ | | |
| × | (6) | Henry is looking forward to going back to Kyoto. |
| ○ | | |

 Emi replied.

**2** Listen to the e-mail and following 6 sentences. Correct the mistakes in each sentence.

音声を聞いて、(7)〜(12) の英文の間違いを訂正しましょう。

| | | |
|---|---|---|
| × | (7) | Emi thought the trip was tiring. |
| ○ | | |
| × | (8) | Emi is bored with studying for tour guide test. |
| ○ | | |
| × | (9) | Emi tells Henry that Mt. Fuji failed to become a World Heritage site. |
| ○ | | |
| × | (10) | Emi doubts that Henry has any reason to come to Japan again. |
| ○ | | |
| × | (11) | Emi explains that washoku is a new food culture in Japan. |
| ○ | | |
| × | (12) | Emi doesn't want to use the photos taken on the journey for Henry's articles. |
| ○ | | |

**3** Read the e-mails from Henry and Emi. Check if your corrections of the sentences in exercise 1 and 2 are right.

ヘンリーとエミのメールを読んで、設問1, 2で文章を正しく訂正できたかどうかを確認しましょう。

Dear Emi,

I just returned to the US and I'm finally relaxing at home. It was a long journey and sometimes I felt tired, but it was worth doing. You've been the greatest assistant to me and proved to be an excellent guide. Without your intensive research, our journey wouldn't have been as successful and enjoyable as it was. Now I have started writing articles for my publisher, and I'm sure they will also appreciate your efforts.

Everything I experienced in Japan was awesome, but Shiretoko and Ogasawara were the best sites for me. Since most guide books focus on the city life of Japan, many people don't get to see the natural beauty that Japan has to offer. I'll be sure to emphasize Japan's natural beauty in my articles. Of course, exploring the cities also gave us a great opportunity to interact with the local people. I'll write about their life, too.

I really wanted to go to Kamakura because I heard you can still see what samurai life was like there. Unfortunately, it's not a World Heritage site, and we didn't have enough time to visit sites outside of our list. Maybe I can visit it next time.

Good luck on your tour guide license test. See you soon.
Sincerely,
Henry

Dear Henry,

It is sad our trip is over, and we're not traveling any more. Our trip was full of excitement. I was relieved to hear you had a safe flight back to the US. I guess you're having a good time with your family now.

I'm busy finishing my studies for the tour guide license, and our trip reminds me of what I learned from the local cultures we visited during our travels. I'm positive it will help me a lot on the test and also for my future guide work.

I have big news about the World Heritage sites in Japan. Mt. Fuji has just been added to the list thanks to the effort of many people. We still have several sites on the waiting list, so you have a good reason to come to Japan, again. Also washoku, traditional dietary cultures of the Japanese has been added to UNESCO's intangible cultural heritage list. Isn't that wonderful?

I'm looking forward to reading your articles. Don't forget to add the pictures you took in Japan, too.

Love,
Emi

## Background information

**4** What other sites are candidates for World Heritage sites in Japan, and which one withdrew? Complete the list of potential World Heritage sites in Japan. Some hints are given.

音声を聞いて、日本の今後の世界遺産について表の (1) 〜 (6) を適切な語句で埋めましょう。

| Name of the place | Location | Status |
|---|---|---|
| (1) | Kanagawa Prefecture | withdrawn |
| Tomioka Silk Mill and Related Industrial Heritage Sites | Gunma Prefecture | listed in 2014 |
| (2) | Shiga Prefecture | preparing to apply |
| (3) | Osaka Prefecture | |
| Asuka-Fujiwara | (4) | |
| (5) | Nagasaki Prefecture | |
| (6) | Niigata Prefecture | |
| Jomon Archeological Site | Tohoku region | |

# Extra activities

# Introduction

**Conversation 1**

Henry Wilckens, a writer for a travel magazine, has just arrived at Kansai International Airport in Japan and is meeting his assistant Emiko Takahashi.

Listen to the conversation and fill in the blanks with the missing words.

**Henry(H)**: Hello. I'm Henry Wilckens of World Travel.
**Emi(E)**: Hi. I'm Emiko Takahashi, and I'll be your (　　) during your (　　) in Japan.
**H**: Nice to meet you, Ms.Takahashi.
**E**: You can call me Emi.
**H**: I see. Please call me Henry. Sorry, I'm (　　) but we had some problems (　　) (　　) of Chicago.
**E**: Oh, don't worry. I was just doing some research (　　)(　　) (　　) we'll be travelling to. I'm trying to get my tour guide (　　), so this will be a great (　　) to test out my knowledge of Japan.
**H**: Great. I'm looking forward to visiting Japanese World Heritage sites and writing some (　　) about them.
**E**: How was your (　　)?
**H**: It was OK, but I'm (　　). I would like to get some rest.
**E**: Alright. I'll call a taxi, and we can go to the hotel.
**H**: We'll go to Tokyo tomorrow morning, right? What time is the train to Tokyo?
**E**: (　　). Six o'clock in the morning.
**H**: Well, we('d) better get to the hotel, so I can be (　　) (　　) tomorrow.
**E**: Alright, I'll go and call the taxi.

**Background information**

What is a World Heritage site? A World Heritage site is a place that is considered culturally or environmentally important to the world, for example buildings, mountains, forests, and cities. These sites are chosen by UNESCO. Every year countries around the world submit to UNESCO places they think are culturally or environmentally significant. UNESCO reviews the list and makes its decision based on several criteria. As of 2013 there are 981 sites listed for 160 countries. World Heritage sites are conserved and protected with money from the World Heritage Fund and private donations. In 1993, Japan was awarded its first sites: Horyuji Temple, Himeji Castle, Yakushima and Shirakami Sanchi.

Answer the questions in complete sentences.
(1) What can become a World Heritage site?
(2) How does UNESCO choose new World Heritage sites?
(3) What were the first World Heritage sites in Japan?
(4) How many World Heritage sites are there in Japan?

Answer each question with your own opinion.
(5) Have you ever visited a World Heritage site in Japan? Which one?
(6) What other World Heritage sites in Japan do you want to visit?
(7) What other Japanese buildings/mountains/forests or cities do you think should be World Heritage sites?

## Conversation 2

Henry and Emi are riding in the taxi to the hotel and are having a discussion about what parts of Japanese culture they like.

Listen to the conversation and fill in the blanks with the missing words.

**Emi(E)**: Oh, look! There is a (           ).
**Henry(H)**: I love old Japanese (           ) and (           ).
**E**: Oh really? What else do you like about Japanese (           )?
**H**: I like a lot of things. For example, I love the (           ) (           ) in Japan. And I have always (           ) (           ) sitting in a hot spring while it's snowing and drinking sake.
**E**: That sounds like a (           ) from a samurai movie.
**H**: Yes, it does. I love samurai movies. I also love the martial arts. How about you? What do you like?
**E**: I like (           ) things like kimonos and tea ceremony. To tell the truth, I really love Japan's nature. I especially like the mountains and forests. And, of course, I love hot springs and sake, too.
**H**: Well, I hope we will see a lot of (           ) on this trip.
**E**: I'm (           ) we will.

## Useful expressions

With your partner, create dialogues for the given situations.

Self-introduction
(1) Partner A is a tour guide and Partner B is a tourist. You are meeting for the first time at Honolulu Airport. Introduce yourselves.
(2) Decide the place or the situation in which you are meeting your partner. Start a conversation with your partner and introduce yourself.

Likes and dislikes
(1) You are at a sushi restaurant with your friend. Talk about your sushi preference with your friend.
(2) You are at a video rental shop with your friend. Decide which movies you will rent together.
(3) Your own idea.

## Unit 1

### Conversation 1

Henry and Emi are heading to Tokyo to take their flight to Shiretoko. It is the first time for Henry to ride on a bullet train.

Listen to the conversation and fill in the blanks with the missing words.

**Emi(E)**: Whew, just (         ) (         ). Here are our seats.
**Henry(H)**: May I sit by the window? I would love to be able to see the Japanese (         ).
**E**: Sure, be my guest.
**H**: Thank you.
**E**: Oh, here comes the (         ) (         ).
**Food cart lady(F)**: Would you care for anything?
**E**: Yes, I'd like some tea and an onigiri, please.
**F**: Alright here you go.

64

**H**: Can I have (          ) tomato juice, please?
**F**: Sorry sir, but we don't have any tomato juice.
**H**: Well, I (          ) I'll just have some green tea and a sandwich please.
**F**: Here you are, sir. Let's see, 300 yen for the sandwich, the tea is 150 yen each and 150 yen for onigiri.
**H**: Here you go.
**F**: Thank you.
**H**: Are sake and beer (          ) on the bullet train, too?
**E**: Yes. (          ) at night, travelers can enjoy drinking alcoholic beverages in the train. When we get to Hokkaido, you can enjoy some sake at the (          ) after sitting in the hot spring.
**H**: That sounds perfect!


## Background information

Shiretoko National Park is located on Hokkaido's Shiretoko Peninsula. The name Shiretoko derives from the Ainu word "sir etok" which means "end of the world". It was designated a Natural World Heritage site in 2005. Because it is one of the least developed areas of Japan, most of the park is not easily accessible by car. Instead, most tourists explore the park either by foot or boat. The park is famous for its beautiful spruce and fir forests, waterfalls, five lakes and being the home of the Ezo brown bears.

Answer the questions in complete sentences.
(1) Why is Shiretoko difficult to get to?
(2) How can you reach most areas of Shiretoko Park?

Answer each question with your own opinion.
(3) From where you live, what is the fastest and cheapest way to travel to Shiretoko?
(4) If you were to explore Shiretoko, where would you like to go and what would you like to see? Make your own tour plan.

## Conversation 2

Henry and Emi are visiting an Ainu museum.

Listen to the conversation and fill in the blanks with the missing words.

**Henry(H)**: Is it true that the Ainu and the Japanese are different people?
**Emi(E)**: Yes, that is true. Some (          ) think the Ainu are the original inhabitants of the Japanese islands.
**H**: What are some differences between the Ainu and the Japanese?
**E**: (          ), Ainu men never shave their beards after a (          ) age, and women wore tattoos around their lips and on their arms.
**H**: Are there any Ainu left in Japan?
**E**: There are a few (          ) Ainu that live in Hokkaido and Russia.
**H**: Can I meet them?
**E**: Yes, there are some (          ) that tourists can visit to learn and experience Ainu culture.
**H**: Great! Let's go then.


## Useful expressions

With your partner, create dialogues for the given situations.

### Asking and giving permission
(1) You and your partner are classmates. You forgot something and want to use your partner's.
(2) You are working at a part-time job. You want to go on a date with your girlfriend / boyfriend instead of working tomorrow. You need to ask your boss for the day off.
(3) Your own idea.

### Ordering food
(1) Partner A is at a café and ordering snack and drink. Partner B is taking Partner A's order.
(2) Partner A is at a restaurant and ordering dinner. Partner B is taking Partner A's order.
(3) Your own idea.

# Unit 2

## Conversation 1

Henry and Emi are visiting Tosho-gu in Nikko.

Listen to the conversation and fill in the blanks with the missing words.

**Henry(H)**: The landscape here is so beautiful. It's (　　　) to believe we are not that far away from Tokyo.
**Emi(E)**: Yes, Tosho-gu is most (　　　) (　　　) its carvings on the buildings.
**H**: Oh, look! There are the three wise monkeys.
**E**: Oh, you have (　　　) (　　　) them?
**H**: Oh, of course! Everyone knows of the three monkeys that see no evil, hear no evil and speak no evil.
**E**: Do you (　　　) why they were carved over that door way?
**H**: No, why?
**E**: That building is called the Shinkyusha, or the stable for royal horses. It was traditionally believed by Japanese that monkeys made good guardians for horses.
**H**: I see. (　　　) (　　　) the sleeping cat we saw earlier? What does it symbolize?
**E**: Peace.
**H**: Look at that carving! What is it?
**E**: The guide book says it's an elephant. The person who drew the design of the elephant had never seen a real elephant, so that one is a (　　　) of his imagination.
**H**: I see.

## Background information

Before becoming the home of Tosho-gu in the 1600's, Nikko was already a pilgrimage center for both Shinto and Buddhist believers and monks. This should be no surprise due to its location. It is surrounded by mountains that are full of hot springs, lakes, waterfalls, and wildlife. Today, Nikko and the surrounding areas are a popular sightseeing destination, power spot, and hiking course. Nikko is enjoyed by both international and Japanese tourists. In 1999, Tosho-gu was added to UNESCO's list of World Heritage sites with other shrines and temples of Nikko.

Answer the questions in complete sentences.
(1) Who traveled to Nikko on pilgrimages?
(2) What is Nikko surrounded by?

Answer each question with your own opinion.
(3) What other sightseeing spots are there in Nikko besides Tosho-gu?

## Conversation 2

Emi explains some of the history of Tosho-gu to Henry.

Listen to the conversation and fill in the blanks with the missing words.

**Henry(H):** So, was Tosho-gu originally built by Tokugawa Hidetada as a shrine for his father Tokugawa Ieyasu?
**Emi(E):** Yes, that's right. But, it was further (         ) on by Ieyasu's grandson Iemitsu.
**H:** Look at all the carvings on the Yomeimon. They're amazing! It must have (         ) (         ) to carve so many perfect sculptures. How long did it take to finish the complex?
**E:** The building was first started in 1617, and it was continually expanded on and rebuilt after fires. But the building is not perfect.
**H:** What do you mean?
**E:** Well, if you look at the Yomeimon's pillars, their designs are going in opposite directions.
**H:** So?
**E:** Well, that represents that the (         ) is not perfect.
**H:** Why (         ) they want that?
**E:** There was a belief that once something became perfect, it started to decline. Therefore, something that is (         ) would last much longer.
**H:** Interesting!

## Useful expressions

With your partner, create dialogues for the given situations.

### Exclaiming admiration
(1) You and your partner have invented a dream machine. Decide the details of the machine and admire it.

(2) Your own idea.

Telling the time and order
(1) Think of your ideal life. Use your imagination. Talk about it with your partner.

# Unit 3

## Conversation 1

Henry and Emi are planning their trip to Ogasawara National Park.

Listen to the conversation and fill in the blanks with the missing words.

**Henry(H)**: The Ogasawara Islands look far away from the (          ) on the map. How far are they?
**Emi(E)**: They are about 1,000 kilometers south of Tokyo, but are still part of Tokyo.
**H**: Really? Can we (          ) there?
**E**: No. They are only accessible by boat. A faster boat called a liner was planned to be (          ) (          ), but they gave up because of its fuel cost.
**H**: I see. How long will it take by the current boat, then?
**E**: More than a day. And that's the problem. I (          ) get seasick.
**H**: Why don't you buy some motion sickness medicine?
**E**: Sometimes that kind of medicine doesn't work at all on me.
**H**: Then, you should (          ) a doctor.
**E**: I guess I don't have any other choice. I will go to see my doctor before we leave.
**H**: Yes, go ahead. (          ) (          ) (          ), I'll learn more about Ogasawara from the book.
**E**: How about going to the library? I'm sure they have some books about Ogasawara written in English.
**H**: OK. I'll (          ) there now.

## Background information

Added in July 2011, Ogasawara is one of Japan's newest additions to UNESCO's list of World Natural Heritage sites. Ogasawara's chain of islands is made up of 30 subtropical and tropical islands. However, people only live on two of the islands, Chichi-jima and Haha-jima. In English, Ogasawara is commonly called "Bonin Islands," which is from the Japanese word "mujin" meaning "no people" or "uninhabited." The Ogasawara Islands are sometimes referred to as the Galapagos of the Orient. The nickname is from the wide variety of plants that have evolved differently on each of the islands. More than 500 plant species grow there, and 43% of them are native to Ogasawara.

Answer the questions in complete sentences.
(1) What does the word uninhabited mean?

Answer each question with your own opinion.
(2) Why have the plants on each island evolved differently from plants on the other islands?
(3) What is a possible threat to the unique species on the Ogasawara Islands?

## Conversation 2

Henry and Emi are talking about Iwo-to on the boat to Ogasawara.

Listen to the conversation and fill in the blanks with the missing words.

**Emi(E):** Kita Iwo-to and Minami Iwo-to are part of the Ogasawara World Heritage site, but (      ), Iwo-to itself isn't listed.
**Henry(H):** But it's too famous to ignore for American people. We call it Iwo Jima.
**E:** Is it (      ) (      ) the Battle of Iwo Jima?
**H:** Yes. Do you know about that?  Starting in February 1945, the American and Japanese armies fought (        ) for more than one month. In the end, America defeated Japan, but many soldiers were killed or hurt.
**E:** How many?
**H:** About 20,000 Japanese soldiers (       ) (       ) 21,000 died, and more than 6,000 American soldiers died, and 22,000 were injured in the tragic battles.
**E:** I've heard that many weapons such as tanks, ships, cannons and aircrafts are still left deserted on the island.
**H:** Yes. Not only the weapons, but the remains of Japanese soldiers are still there resting (         ). And the survivors from both sides of the battle met and conducted a memorial service together for the fortieth and fiftieth anniversary of

the battle.

**E**: I see. Since ordinary people are not allowed to land on Iwo-to, we should pray for peace from here.

**H**: Yes. And I'm glad that we are friends now and are travelling (      ) on these beautiful islands.

## Useful expressions

With your partner, create dialogues for the given situations.

### Giving advice
(1) Think of the ways to improve your English. Tell your partner and ask for his/her opinion.
(2) Your own idea.

### Asking the distance and necessary time
(1) Research secluded places in Japan. Explain how to get there to your partner.

# Unit 4

## Conversation 1

Henry and Emi are looking at a group of houses in Gokayama in Toyama Prefecture.

Listen to the conversation and fill in the blanks with the missing words.

**Henry(H)**: Wow, those houses have interesting-looking roofs. The angle of the roof is really (      )!

**Emi(E)**: It is called gassho-zukuri, and the angle is said to be between 45 and 60 degrees.

**H**: Gassho? What does it (      )?

**E**: It means clasping your hands in prayer.

**H**: I see. But it looks like a (      ) block house, with a pyramid on top.

**E**: Yes. The basic (          ) of the gassho-zukuri house is different from that of ordinary Japanese houses. An ordinary Japanese house has pillars up to the attic, and those pillars and walls (          ) the first floor space into small rooms.
**H**: Yes?
**E**: But here, they construct the first floor and then they put a roof on top of it.
**H**: I see. That's the (          ) why there are wide spaces on both the first floor and in the attic.
**E**: Yes. The attic is usually two or three stories high.
**H**: (          ) do they use the space (          )?
**E**: I've heard that they used it for silk culture in summer and paper making in winter. They also made gunpowder.
**H**: How (          )!

## Background information

The villages of Shirakawa-go and Gokayama in Gifu and Toyama Prefecture, which have preserved the traditional way of living in gassho-zukuri houses, were listed on the UNESCO World Heritage Site for culture in 1995. Surrounded by mountains, they have heavy snowfall during winter. Sometimes the snowfall is over 2 meters deep. Before roadways around the area were developed, the area had been "isolated" especially in winter. At the end of the 19th century, they had more than 1,800 gassho-zukuri houses. However, the number of the houses dropped sharply in the middle of the 20th century. A group of people in the region started a conservation movement in the 1960's. Thanks to the efforts of the people and the areas' local governments, this unique landscape has been preserved. Today, more than 1.5 million tourists come to visit the area each year, where less than 3,000 people live.

Answer the questions in complete sentences.
(1) What do they have in Shirakawa-go and Gokayama in winter?
(2) What was the area of Shirakawa-go and Gokayama like before roadways were developed?
(3) Do you want to live in a gassho-zukuri house? Think of the advantages and disadvantages of living in a gassho-zukuri house.
(4) What other famous architecture do you want to preserve in Japan?

## Conversation 2

Henry and Emi are looking at the houses again in Gokayama.

Listen to the conversation and fill in the blanks with the missing words.

**Emi(E)**: The roof material is called "kaya" and they need to re-thatch the roof once (　　　) 20 or 30 years.
**Henry(H)**: How much (　　　) do they need to re-thatch the roof?
**E**: Well, in the past, they did it (　　) (　　) (　　), and it took a lot of time to complete. If they did it in a day or two, more than 100 people would be needed.
**H**: That many? Who were those people? It must have cost a lot of money to (　　　) them.
**E**: Yes, if you hired the people, it would cost more than 30 million yen.
**H**: Then, were they all (　　　)?
**E**: Well, traditionally, all the villages had mutual cooperating groups named "yui", and in "yui" they helped (　　) (　　) to maintain their community.
**H**: Are "yui" decreasing?
**E**: Yes. The number of gassho-zukuri houses has decreased a lot, so "yui" are also decreasing.
**H**: That's (　　　). Finding time to work together can be very difficult.
**E**: Yes. So in many cases, re-thatching is done by a local forestry cooperative here in Gokayama.

## Useful expressions

With your partner, create dialogues for the given situations.

If …(conditional)
(1) Imagine you are the opposite gender. Tell your partner what you would do if you were a man or a woman.
(2) Imagine you were a teacher. Tell your partner how you would teach in the classroom.

# Unit 5

### Conversation 1

Henry and Emi are window shopping in Kawaramachi area in Kyoto.

Listen to the conversation and fill in the blanks with the missing words.

**Henry(H)**: I need to pick up something for my (          ) living in Hawaii. Do you have any good ideas?
**Emi(E)**: Well, the first thing that comes to (          ) is sweets. Japanese sweets in Kyoto are really good.
**H**: But can you send them overseas?
**E**: Sorry, you can't. How old is your niece? What does she like?
**H**: She is 13. She likes (          ) princess-like things a lot.
**E**: Then, what about Nishijin silk fabric? It's intricate and gorgeous.
**H**: The one for Kimono and Obi? I know it's beautiful, but too expensive. I can't (          ) it.
**E**: Kiyomizu ceramic ware is also famous. Most of them are (          ) and beautifully colored.
**H**: Yeah, but aren't they fragile? I don't want it to get broken during delivery. I noticed there are a lot of wooden craft shops. How about the comb we just saw in the (          )?
**E**: Well, usually, it's not a good idea to give a comb as a gift in Japan.
**H**: (          ) (          )?
**E**: Comb is "kushi" in Japanese, and "ku" means agony and "shi" means death.
**H**: Oh, no, I don't want to give agony and death to my lovely niece.
**E**: Look at the folding fans there! Aren't they (          )?
**H**: Yeah, very cute. A folding fan is light enough to send. I'll (          ) (          ) (          ) at the one with a black cat. She loves cats and collects things with cats. I'm sure she'll like it.

### Background information

Kyoto was the cultural and religious center after it became the political capital in 794. Even though Kyoto was destroyed by many wars and fires, Japanese traditional culture matured there over the centuries. Now, Kyoto Prefecture is said to have more than 2,400 temples and shrines. Among them, 17 properties including one temple in Shiga Prefecture were designated as a UNESCO World Heritage Site in 1994. Three out of 17 are shrines, 13 are temples, and one is a castle. They attract many tourists from in and outside of Japan because each of them embodies the period when it was constructed. Goju-no To, or the five-tiered pagoda, of To-ji Temple, for example, is 57 meters high, which is the tallest pagoda in Japan. Ryoanji Temple, which was built in 1450, is also famous for its garden with 15 stones.

Answer the questions in complete sentences.
(1) How has Kyoto been destroyed throughout history?
(2) Why are many tourists attracted to Kyoto?

Answer each question with your own opinion.
(3) Have you ever been to Kyoto? How many times have you been there? What did you see there?
(4) What image do you have of Kyoto?

## Conversation 2

Henry and Emi are visiting Kozanji Temple, one of the temples listed as a UNESCO World Heritage site.

Listen to the conversation and fill in the blanks with the missing words.

**Emi(E)**: Japanese traditional culture such as tea ceremony and (　　) (　　) were developed by the political elite especially during the Muromachi and later periods in Kyoto.
**Henry(H)**: I read in a brochure that this temple has the oldest tea (　　) in Japan. Was the tea tree from China?
**E**: Yes. The founder of this temple, Myoue, planted the tea seeds given by Eisai, a monk who returned from Sung during the Kamakura period. They (　　) well, and the habit of drinking tea came to be popular first among Buddhist monks and (　　) samurai.
**H**: Interesting! It is like coffee. It is said that coffee was (　　) drunk by monks in Ethiopia to keep them awake.
**E**: Yeah, Japanese tea might have been used as (　　), too.
**H**: Then, how did drinking tea become the elegant tea ceremony we have today?

E: In the 15th and 16th century, it came to be associated with Zen Buddhism (          ) and gradually formed as what we know as tea ceremony.

H: I see.

E: If you are interested, why don't you take a (          )? I'm sure they have a short trial lesson for tourists.

H: Good idea, but maybe some other time. I want to see (          ) temples and shrines in Kyoto now.

## Useful expressions

With your partner, create dialogues for the given situations.

Refusal
(1) Your partner wants you to do his/her homework, but you don't want to do it. Tell your partner that you will not do it and the reason why.
(2) Your own idea.

# Unit 6

## Conversation 1

Henry and Emi are now in Nara visiting the remains of Heijo-kyo, which was restored recently.

Listen to the conversation and fill in the blanks with the missing words.

**Henry(H)**: It is (          ). Those buildings really look like the ones I saw in Korea last year.

**Emi(E)**: Oh, in what way?

H: Well, the general atmosphere of the buildings, the shape of the roof, the ornaments on the roof and the colors. The combination of red, gold and green reminds me of a Korean palace.

E: I guess the (          ) in Nara period was strongly influenced by China.

H: Really? It was more than 1200 year ago, and did they have any (          ) with

Chinese culture?

E: Yes. They sent "kentoshi", or official (　　　) to China. Those people came back with a lot of books on Buddhism, sculptures, and arts and crafts.

H: Wow, it must have been (　　　) to cross the sea.

E: Indeed. They made a very hard journey on a small boat. Some were (　　　) (　　　) by the stormy ocean, and some tried to come or go many times and failed in the end.

H: I'm surprised that they would cross the ocean on a wooden boat with just a few sails. Nara was connected with China, then.

E: Actually, not just with China. Nara was the (　　　) of the Silk Road.

H: Wow! The Silk Road? That led all the way to Persia.

## Background information

Nara was the capital of Japan from 710 to 794, which was called "Heijo-kyo." The political and cultural foundation of Japan was established during this period. Every monarch of Heijo-kyo was interested in absorbing foreign cultures, especially Chinese culture. Strongly influenced by Buddhism, many temples were built. Shinto shrines were also constructed to protect the country. One of the major temples which represents Heijo-kyo period is Todai-ji Temple with the Great Buddha. Nara was designated a World Heritage site for culture in 1998 and is known as "Historic Monuments of Ancient Nara."

Answer the questions in complete sentences.
(1) What was the capital of Japan called during the Nara period?
(2) Why were many shrines built during the Nara period?

Answer each question with your own opinion.
(3) How big is the Great Buddha in Todaiji-Temple?
(4) What other sites are possible candidates for World Heritage sites in Nara Prefecture?

## Conversation 2

Henry and Emi are walking down the street in Nara and discussing the life of the ancient Japanese people.

Listen to the conversation and fill in the blanks with the missing words.

**Henry(H):** I (            ) how the people during the Nara period spent their daily life.
**Emi(E):** Well, information about the way people lived in the palace has been gradually revealed thanks to excavations.
**H:** That was a long time ago, was their life (            )?
**E:** Not at all. Actually, it was kind of modern. The treasures kept in the treasure house of Tōdai-ji show that they used (            ) just like us.
**H:** Really? Didn't they use tatami mats?
**E:** No. The emperor sat on a chair when he met court. He slept on a wooden bed with tatami-mats on it. They also had carpets on the floor, too.
**H:** Did the government (            ) work in an office like us, too?
**E:** Yes. They did some work at a desk and (            ) their paperwork in a chest.
**H:** Interesting!

### Useful expressions

With your partner, create dialogues for the given situations.

Expressing astonishment
(1) Think of the news which surprised you recently. Talk about it with your partner.
(2) Your own idea.

# Unit 7

### Conversation 1

Henry and Emi are walking on the path of Kumano Kodo.

Listen to the conversation and fill in the blanks with the missing words.

**Henry(H):** So, this is one of the pilgrimage routes that leads to Kumano-sanzan, or a (            ) of three shrines.

**Emi(E)**: Yes. There are many routes that connect the (          ) places in this area, and the one we're walking on now was popular among lay travelers from Kyoto.

**H**: Lay travelers? I thought it was only monks who did ascetic practices.

**E**: Originally, they were. But in 1090 the ex-emperor Shirakawa visited Kumano for the first time and returned 9 times after that.

**H**: 9 times!

**E**: Don't be surprised. The most (          ) visitor was the ex-emperor Goshirakawa who came 33 times, followed by the ex-emperor Gotoba with 28 pilgrimages. The ex-emperor Toba, who came 21 times, took third place.

**H**: Wow, they came (          ) every year!

**E**: Yes. And that made the trip to Kumano very popular, first among the (          ) and later among the ordinary people.

**H**: Why did the ex-emperors visit this area so many times? They must have had some (          ).

**E**: Of course they had religious reasons, but (          ) (          ) to that, a trip to Kumano had a special meaning.

**H**: Hmm, I guess I know the reason. It must have been a kind of political parade to show off their power.

**E**: Yes, that's right. And later, it would be the only trip in a lifetime for common people.

## Background information

The "Sacred Sites and Pilgrimage Routes of the Kii Mountain Range", including Kumano Kodo, were registered as a UNESCO World Heritage site in 2004. It consists of three sacred locations "Kumano Sanzan," "Yoshino and Omine" and "Koyasan." The site area covers 495.3 hectares making it the largest Cultural Heritage site in Japan. This area is also known for its heavy rainfalls around the year. In 2011 the area was heavily damaged by intense rainfall and mudslides caused by a typhoon. Near Kumano Hongu Taisha a large-scale mudslide buried 50 meters of the Kumano Kodo. The Nachi-no-Otaki waterfall suffered damage, too. The rocks in the basin were carried away by the vast amount of water from the mountains, which resulted in changing the shape of the waterfall's basin.

Answer the questions in complete sentences.
(1) What did a typhoon cause in 2011?
(2) When do they usually have heavy rain in Kumano?

Answer each question with your opinion.
(3) What damage do typhoons often cause?
(4) Are you interested in hiking in the Kumano area?

## Conversation 2

Henry and Emi are looking at a banner near a torii at Kumano Hongu Taisha.

Listen to the conversation and fill in the blanks with the missing words.

**Henry(H)**: Is the crow on that banner some type of (　　　)?
**Emi(E)**: Yes, it is said to be a symbol of the sun, and it appears in Japanese myths.
**H**: What did it do in the myths?
**E**: When the first emperor Jinmu came to (　　　) the East, he and his army got lost in the mountains. A crow appeared and led them to Yamato where the emperor Jinmu (　　　) the capital.
**H**: Hmm… The crow has three legs. I think I've seen a three-legged crow (　　　) before.
**E**: At the soccer game?
**H**: Maybe.
**E**: Actually, the three-legged crow is called Yatagarasu. It is a symbol of Japan Football Association.
**H**: I see. But why has it come to be a (　　　) (　　　) (　　　) in Japan?
**E**: The three reasons are well known.
**H**: I got it. The crow will lead you to victory, right?
**E**: Yes. And the founder of Japan's modern football league was from this area. (　　　), an expert of kemari, a ball game played by aristocrats in the Heian period, came to Kumano many times.
**H**: I see. The crow can help someone because it will lead them to victory. Now, let's go (　　　) the shrine.
**E**: OK.

## Useful expressions

With your partner, create dialogues for the given situations.

must/might have

(1) Think of a historical hero. Describe what you think his / her live was like using "must/might have."
(2) Your own idea.

# Unit 8

## Conversation 1

Henry and Emi are touring Himeji Castle in Hyogo Prefecture.

Listen to the conversation and fill in the blanks with the missing words.

**Henry(H)**: This place is awesome. It feels like I'm in a samurai movie.
**Emi(E)**: Yes, it does have that (          ).
**H**: I wonder what it would have been like to be a samurai in old Japan.
**E**: While some high ranking samurai had easy lives, the (          ) had very strict and (          ) lives.
**H**: How so?
**E**: Well, after the Sengoku Period, or the Warring States Period, Japan's feudal system became very rigid.
**H**: How is that?
**E**: After the Sengoku Period, almost all the castles were (          ) (          ). And all the lords' or daimyo families had to live in Edo while the daimyo was required to live there every other year.
**H**: Wow! That is strict. Well, what about the (          ) of society? What was (          ) of them?
**E**: Well, there were basically four classes: warriors or samurai, farmers, craftsmen and merchants.
**H**: It's pretty much the same as the European feudal system. But why aren't the farmers (          ) (          ) (          )?
**E**: Well, everyone was supposed to contribute to society. Samurai had to enforce laws and protect the people. Farmers had to produce food for society.
**H**: How about craftsmen?
**E**: They were expected to make tools and other things that the samurai and farmers needed. Merchants bought and sold products made by farmers and craftsmen.

However, they did nothing productive for society.
H: I see. That's why merchants were at the bottom of the (         ).

## Background information

Himeji Castle, also known as "White Egret Castle" or "White Heron Castle" was one of Japan's first UNESCO World Heritage sites with its inclusion in 1993. Himeji Castle is Japan's largest and most visited castle and is considered one of the country's finest castles. Unlike many of Japan's castles, Himeji has remained relatively intact for 400 years, surviving the bombing of Himeji city during World War II and the 1995 Great Hanshin Earthquake. Himeji Castle's history goes back over 679 years with the first castle built in 1333. The original castle was taken down and rebuilt in 1346. In 1581 the castle was taken over by Toyotomi Hideyoshi and then passed on to Ikeda Terumasa for his support of Tokugawa Ieyasu in the Battle of Sekigahara. From 1601 to 1609 Ikeda tore down and rebuilt it as the present castle.

Answer the questions in complete sentences.
(1) What is Himeji Castle known as?

Answer each question with your own opinion.
(2) Have you ever been to Himeji Castle?
(3) What other castles have you ever been to?

## Conversation 2

Henry notices a rack of weapons when Henry and Emi are exploring Himeji Castle and starts explaining how to make katana.

Listen to the conversation and fill in the blanks with the missing words.

**Henry(H)**: I would love to buy a katana, but they are too (         ).
**Emi(E)**: Like (         ) (         ) ?
**H**: Anywhere from 4,000 to 10,000 dollars.
**E**: Wow, why are they that expensive?
**H**: Well, it takes a lot of time and effort to make an (         ) katana.
**E**: How is a katana made?

H: Well, it's (        ) but I will try to summarize it for you.
E: OK.
H: First, a smith makes two blocks of steel from some pieces of preselected steel.
E: (        ) does he use two pieces?
H: One piece is made of (        ) steel that will be used for the outside. The other block is a (        ) steel for the inside of the sword.
E: Then does the smith fold the steel?
H: Yes. A smith will usually fold a block of steel 10 or 13 times.
E: Is the sword (        ) after that?
H: No. Next, he hammers the steel into the basic shape of the sword.
E: I see. How does the sword get that wavy line on the (        ) then?
H: That is near the end. The smith applies some wet clay to the sword with a thin layer near the cutting edge and a thicker layer near the back.
E: Yeah?
H: Then, he heats the metal again. After that he dips the whole sword into water.
E: Wow! That is (        ) (        ) (        ) work. Thanks for teaching me.

## Useful expressions

With your partner, create dialogues for the given situations.

Expressing obligation and need
(1) If you were the principle of the high school you graduated from, what would the students have to do? Think of new rule for the school.
(2) If you were the teacher of this class, what would the students be expected to do? Think of some rules for the class.

# Unit 9

## Conversation 1

Emi and Henry are visiting the Atomic-Bomb Dome.

Listen to the conversation and fill in the blanks with the missing words.

**Emi(E)**: I think you've seen the Atomic-Bomb Dome before.

**Henry(H)**: Yeah. I (          ) I once saw a picture of it in a history textbook.

**E**: Now that you can see it with your own eyes, how do you feel?

**H**: I'm speechless. It's (          ) to imagine that everyone standing here was instantly killed on August 6, 1945, but this building survived the dropping of the A-bomb. That's (          )!

**E**: I agree. (          ) standing for more than 65 years, it looks as if it'll fall apart at any moment.

**H**: It's amazing! I feel that the dome's ability to remain standing represents the (          ) (          ) of Hiroshima's citizens.

**E**: I've heard people in Hiroshima (          ) to preserve the dome, not just as a memorial of the first dropping of an atomic bomb. It is also a symbol of perseverance and peace.

**H**: I'm so glad I got a chance to visit this (          ) place.

**E**: Me, too. This is a (          ) for all people visiting Hiroshima.

### Background information

The Hiroshima Peace Memorial (Genbaku Dome) was the only structure left standing in the area after the first atomic bomb used as a weapon exploded on August 6, 1945. The atomic bomb, codenamed Little Boy, exploded 600 meters above Shima Surgical Clinic with the power of 12 kilotons of dynamite. The fireball created by the nuclear reaction was 370 meters in diameter and reached temperatures of 3,980 °C. Severe structural damage was about 3.2 km in diameter with the resulting firestorm burning down everything within 11 km². An estimated 130,000 to 150,000, or 30% of Hiroshima's population, died in the initial blast. Because the hypocenter was over the medical district of the city, over 90% of its doctors and nurses were killed along with the destruction of the city's medical supplies. Through the efforts of many people, including those of the city of Hiroshima, the Hiroshima Peace Memorial has been preserved in the same state as it was immediately after the bombing. Not only is it a stark and powerful symbol of the most destructive force ever created by humankind, it also expresses the hope for world peace and the ultimate elimination of all nuclear weapons.

Answer the questions in complete sentences.
(1) What other structures besides the Hiroshima Peace Memorial were left after the first atomic bomb exploded in Hiroshima in 1945?

Answer each question with your own opinion.
(2) Have you ever been to the Hiroshima Peace Memorial? If yes, how did you feel?
(3) Go to the Hiroshima Peace Memorial Museum website. Browse the site and the Hiroshima Peace Database. Summarize and discuss what you learn with your partner.

## Conversation 2

Emi and Henry visit the Peace Museum for the first time.

Listen to the conversation and fill in the blanks with the missing words.

**Emi(E)**: Wow, the Peace Museum was so moving.
**Henry(H)**: Yeah. But it will (     ) (     ) (     ) for me to be able to put into words how I feel about everything we saw in the museum.
**E**: Visiting the museum made me (     ) how little I've thought of war in my daily life.
**H**: In school we learned about the dropping of the atomic bomb on Hiroshima, but the museum gave me a better (     ) of the suffering it caused civilians.
**E**: I agree.
**H**: You could see that many of the visitors to the (     ) were shocked and saddened by the photographs of the victims of radiation burns. I was amazed by the photographs of the destroyed city.
**E**: The survivors' drawings of their experience were the most painful for me to look at.
**H**: Yes, they give us a glimpse of the victims' feelings of horror, loneliness and pain.
**E**: It makes me angry knowing that some people are still (     ) from the effects of the atomic bomb.
**H**: Me, too. But hopefully those drawings and photographs will continue to teach people the horrible price of (     ) (     ).

## Useful expressions

With your partner, create dialogues for the given situations.

Expressing your feeling of obligation with causative words
(1) Think of 5 good things that make you have positive feelings. Talk about it with your partner using the expressions "… makes me …"
(2) Ask your partner what makes him/her have negative feelings, like being

disappointed, depressed, etc.

# Unit 10

### Conversation 1

Henry and Emi are visiting Itsukushima Shrine in Miyajima.

Listen to the conversation and fill in the blanks with the missing words.

**Henry(H)**: Look at that torii gate! It's gigantic! The people standing around the gate look so (        ).
**Emi(E)**: It is called Miyajima Torii which is one of the most popular tourist (        ) in Japan. It is about 16 meters high, and the top beam is 24 meters long.
**H**: Hmm, that big, huh? The white walls and orange pillars of this shrine make me really (        ) (        ) I'm in Japan.
**E**: I know what you mean.
**H**: Yeah. And the guidebook says this is an island of the gods. I can practically feel its (        ).
**E**: Did you know there are three ponds at this shrine that according to legend appeared in one night when the buildings were first (        )?
**H**: Three ponds? The shrine is on the sea and has ponds? Where are they?
**E**: Since the tide is (        ) now, you can see the one called Kagami-no ike, or Mirror Pond, when you go down the (        ).
**H**: Great! The brochure also says the view of the gate changes during a single day. Is that right?
**E**: That's right. The (        ) gate appears to be floating in the water during high tide.
**H**: I'd really like to see the "floating gate."
**E**: Me, too. Henry, we still have time for (        ) tide. Can you wait for three hours or more?
**H**: No problem. We can't (        ) this chance. Let's go and see the pond and other buildings of the shrine.
**E**: Sure. Then we'll go around and pick up some souvenirs and get back here when it's high tide.

## Background information

Itsukushima Shrine along with all of Miyajima Island in Hiroshima, was added to UNESCO's list of World Heritage sites in 1996. The island is traditionally considered the home of gods, especially the sea and storm god Susanoo no Mikoto and his three daughters. Because the island is considered the sacred home of the gods, the shrine was built over the water so that people could visit it without dirtying the gods' home. Even now, residents dying from sicknesses and women about to give birth are supposed to move to the mainland to avoid polluting the shrine, since blood and death are supposed to displease the Shinto gods. Besides Itsukushima Shrine the island is famous for Miyajima Torii, or Grand Gate that seems to float on the ocean during high tide, Senjokaku (The Hall of 1,000 Tatami Mats), a five-story pagoda, and Momijidani Park.

Answer the questions in complete sentences.
(1) What things are supposed to displease the Shinto gods?

Answer each question with your own opinion.
(2) If you were to build something that floats on water, what would you make?
(3) What Shinto gods do you know? Name some and explain what they are gods of.

## Conversation 2

Henry and Emi are walking around Miyajima.

Listen to the conversation and fill in the blanks with the missing words.

**Henry(H)**: Well, we got some time to (          ), so do you have any good spots in mind, Emi?
**Emi(E)**: Yeah. I've read there's an amazing attraction on the island.
**H**: What is it? Another god's building (        ) (         )?
**E**: Not really. It's a short trip to the top of a low mountain called Mount Misen, where we can enjoy a nice (        ). We can go there by the ropeway.
**H**: Sounds (        ).
**E**: OK, good. Let's go and buy a ticket for the ropeway.
    (10 min. later)
**E**: It is a bit surprising that the (         ) is rather expensive.
**H**: Geez, a round trip ticket is 1,800 yen! Do we have any other choice?

E: Let me see… yes, the guidebook says you can (          ) up to the mountain. It'll take 90 minutes or so. What do you think?

H: Umm… I'd like to (          ) my money for dinner tonight. Is it OK, Emi?

E: Definitely! I'm with you, Henry.

(Some 90 minutes later)

H: We finally (          ) (          ) to the top, Emi.

E: Yeah. We did it. But I'm all sweaty. Look at my sweaty shirt, Henry.

H: I've got the (          ) problem.

E: Let me take a drink of water before getting the (          ) views.

H: Emi, hurry! Come here. The amazing views are right in front of us!

E: Wow! It is a 360 degree view of Honshu and the neighboring islands of the Inland Sea.

**Useful expressions**

With your partner, create dialogues for the given situations.

Expressions for sequence

(1) Think about when you were in high school. Find something different from what you do now. Explain it to your partner using sequence words such as before, after, and so on.

(2) Imagine your life after finishing college. Explain it to your partner using sequence words, such as before, after, and so on.

# Unit 11

**Conversation 1**

Henry and Emi are about to hike through the sugi forest of Yakushima.

Listen to the conversation and fill in the blanks with the missing words.

**Emi(E)**: Some of the trees in Yakushima are (          ) 2,000 years old. The oldest and biggest is the Jomonsugi.

**Henry(H)**: Oh! I would love to see that.

**E**: Don't worry, we're (       ) that way now.

**H**: Oh, no! It's (       ) to rain. (Henry rummages through his back bag.) Crud, I think I forgot my raincoat at the inn.

**E**: (Laughing.) I noticed you left it on the chair in the lobby, so I packed it for you.

**H**: Thanks so much. I hope I didn't forget to pack anything else. Let's see.

**E**: Did you (       ) your flashlight and head light?

**H**: Check. I have both. I also have my emergency whistle that has a compass, match case, mirror and magnifying glass.

**E**: Good, I have my cell phone, a (       ) first aid kit and a chocolate bar in my backpack.

**H**: Did you bring your hiking poles?

**E**: Hiking poles?

**H**: Yes, hiking poles. They keep your knees from getting tired when you are climbing up and down the mountains. I have two (       ) so I'll let you use one.

**E**: Thanks!

**H**: Let's see, I also have snacks.

**E**: Well, it sounds like we are ready.

**H**: Wait… Good. I didn't forget an (       ) pair of socks.

**E**: What?

**H**: You should always keep your feet warm and dry, so you don't catch a cold or hurt your feet.

**E**: (Laughing.) You sound as if you've climbed Mt. Fuji. Anyways, let's go see that Jomonsugi before it gets (       ) (       ).

## Background information

Yakushima became a World Heritage site in 1993. Yakushima is one of the Osumi islands located on the northern tip of the Ryukyu island chain. Yakushima is best known for its cryptomeria, also called sugi trees. Among them, Jomonsugi is the oldest and the biggest at 25.3 meters tall and 16.2 meters in circumference and is over 2,000 years old. Yakushima is also famous for being the wettest place in Japan. It rains twice as much as the average Japanese rainfall. The forest is visited by around 300,000 tourists every year. After the forests became protected, tourism has become a major source of income for the locals. Besides its forests, the island is also famous for being the largest nesting ground of the loggerhead sea turtle in the North Pacific and being the southernmost place in Japan where there is snow on the mountains.

Answer the questions in complete sentences.
(1) Where is Yakushima located?
(2) Besides sugi trees, what is Yakushima famous for?

Answer each question with your own opinion.
(3) What is the most economical way to go to Yakushima from where you are now?
(4) If you had a chance to go to Yakushima, what would like to do there?

## Conversation 2

Henry and Emi have arrived at Jomonsugi and start to discuss tree worship around the world.

Listen to the conversation and fill in the blanks with the missing words.

**Henry(H)**: It's (　　　) than I imagined. It hurts my neck just looking at the top of it.
**Emi(E)**: Yeah, it's (　　　).
**H**: It looks like some old giant just standing there. I'm surprised it doesn't have a shimenawa around it.
**E**: Well, the guide book does say that even without a shimenawa the Yakusugi were (　　　) as sacred trees.
**H**: Yeah.
**E**: Oh, here is something else. It says that Jomonsugi was partnered with a giant kauri tree in New Zealand called TaneMahuta, or "The Lord of the Forrest." The tree is (　　　) a god by the Maori people.
**H**: You mean Jomonsugi and the kauri tree in New Zealand have a partnership?
**E**: Yes. The project is called "The Family of Ancient Trees."
**H**: It seems like sacred trees are a (　　　) thing. There is the tree of life in many mythologies.
**E**: You mean all (　　　) (　　　) (　　　)?
**H**: Yes. The Tree of knowledge in Judaism and Christianity, Banyan and Peepal trees in Hinduism, the Bodhi tree in Buddhism and the Christmas tree of Germanic mythology.
**E**: I guess since they provide shelter, food, fuel and live so long, it's not (　　　) that people around the world consider them sacred.

## Useful expressions

With your partner, create dialogues for the given situations.

### Comparatives and superlatives
(1) Compare yourself with your partner. Find some differences. Talk about those differences with your partner using comparatives.

### Similarities
(1) Draw a simple picture. First, draw a circle. Second, draw two dots in the circle. Then, draw a line which crosses the circle. What does it look like? Show your partner and ask what it looks like.

# Unit 12

## Conversation 1

Henry and Emi are on a plane flying over Okinawa.

Listen to the conversation and fill in the blanks with the missing words.

**Emi(E)**: We are (      ) (      ) arrive.
**Henry(H)**: Look at the beautiful sea! It's such a beautiful emerald blue.
**E**: Yes. As you know, Okinawa is one of the most popular resort sites in Japan. Over 5 million people visit there (      ) (      ).
**H**: Yeah. But Okinawa has a complicated history, I heard. Wasn't it an (      ) country?
**E**: Yes. It was the Kingdom of Ryukyu for 450 years until the Meiji Government created Okinawa Prefecture in 1879. Even though it was independent, the Kingdom of Ryukyu was strongly influenced and controlled by both the Ming and Qing Dynasty and the Satsuma Domain.
**H**: Then, it was also occupied by the US after World War II.
**E**: Yes. Just before the war (      ) in 1945, they had severe battles between the US Army and that of Japan in Okinawa for 3 months from March to June.
**H**: I know. More than 200,000 people including American and Japanese soldiers and Japanese civilian people (      ) (      ).

E: Yes, and at that time Shuri-jo, or the main castle of the Ryukyu Kingdom, was completely destroyed.
H: But some parts of the Shuri-jo have been restored, right?
E: Yes. Since Okinawa was returned to Japan in 1972, people in Okinawa have been trying to restore the ruins. You can visit (      ) (      ) (      ) now.
H: It makes you appreciate our peaceful society that allows us to travel together.
E: Indeed.

## Background information

Gusuku sites, or the castles and related properties of the Kingdom of Ryukyu, were designated World Heritage sites in 2000. The castles of Okinawa were called "gusuku" in the Okinawan language. Among the five "gusuku" on the UNESCO list, Shuri-jo was the most important castle of the Ryukyu Kingdom. It was used as the central government office and royal residence. It was destroyed in the Battle of Okinawa and reconstructed in 1992. It is the only castle in Okinawa that has been reconstructed. The other castles remain only ruins. Shikina-en, one of the 4 properties of the Ryukyu Kingdom on the UNESCO list, was constructed in the end of the 18th century. It was used as the second residence of the Ryukyu kings. It was also completely destroyed in the Battle of Okinawa of 1945, but restored in 2000.

Answer the questions in complete sentences.
(1) How many "gusuku" are listed on the World Heritage site list?
(2) What happened to Shikinaen in 1945?

Answer each question with your own opinion.
(3) Have you ever been to Okinawa before? If you had a/another chance to go to Okinawa, where would you like to go? What would you like to do?

## Conversation 2

Henry and Emi are walking on the main street in Naha.

Listen to the conversation and fill in the blanks with the missing words.

**Emi(E)**: Our trip is (      ). Why don't we have an Okinawan food party tonight?
**Henry(H)**: Great idea! I heard that through China's influence, traditionally,

Okinawans believe that food is the best medicine for (    ) illness.

E: Yes, and Okinawa is well known as the prefecture of longevity.
H: I noticed that elderly people look happy working here and there.
E: They eat various kinds of food good for their health. They (    ) use konbu when cooking and eat a pig from its head to tail.
H: Whole? Not just meat, but other parts of the pig?
E: Yes, (    ). Actually, I've eaten ears and hands of pigs several times before.
H: Really?
E: Yes, they are delicious and perfect for your skin-care.
H: Interesting. I'm lucky to have a chance to eat those (    ) foods here.
E: I'm sure you'll like them. I also recommend tofu made from peanuts and goya chanpuru, or a (    ) fry dish made with goya, a bitter melon.
H: My mouth is watering. I can't wait (    ) (    ). Let's go now!
E: Sure. I'm really happy to guide you to my favorite restaurant in Okinawa.

## Useful expressions

With your partner, create dialogues for the given situations.

Commenting on someone's statement.
(1) Think of effective ways to improve one's English. Explain the steps your partner. Your partner will comment on your instructions.
(2) Think of the things you are good at. Choose one thing and teach your partner the steps needed to become good at it. Your partner will comment on your instructions.

# Epilogue

Emi received an e-mail from Henry.

Listen to the e-mail anf fill in the blanks with the missing words.

Dear Emi,

I just returned to the US and I'm (          ) relaxing at home. It was a long journey and sometimes I felt (          ) but it was worth doing. You've been the greatest assistant to me and proved to be an excellent guide. Without your (          ) research, our journey wouldn't have been as successful and enjoyable as it was. Now I have started writing articles for my publisher, and I'm sure they will also (          ) your efforts.

Everything I experienced in Japan was awesome, but Shiretoko and Ogasawara were the best sites for me. Since most guide books (          ) (          ) the city life of Japan, many people don't get to see the natural beauty that Japan has to offer. I'll be sure to (          ) Japan's natural beauty in my articles. Of course, exploring the cities also gave us a great opportunity to interact with the local people. I'll write about their life, too.

I really wanted to go to Kamakura because I heard you can still see what samurai life was like there. (          ), it's not a World Heritage site, and we didn't have enough time to visit sites outside of our list. Maybe I can visit it next time.

Good luck on your tour guide license test. See you soon.
    (          ),
Henry

Emi replied.

Dear Henry,

It is (          ) our trip is over, and we're not traveling any more. Our trip was full of excitement. I was (          ) to hear you had a safe flight back to the US. I guess you're having a good time with your family now.

I'm busy finishing my studies for the tour guide license, and our trip reminds me of what I learned from the local cultures we visited during our travels. I'm (          ) it will help me a lot on the test and also for my future guide work.

I have big news about the World Heritage sites in Japan. Mt. Fuji has just been added to the list (         ) (            ) the effort of many people. We still have several sites on the waiting list, so you have a good reason to come to Japan, again. Also washoku, traditional dietary cultures of the Japanese has been added to UNESCO's intangible (          ) heritage list. Isn't that wonderful?

I'm looking forward to reading your articles. Don't forget to add the pictures you took in Japan, too.

Love,
Emi

## Background information

As of 2013, there are twelve locations on Japan's tentative list of potential World Heritage sites. Kamakura was on the list for many years but was withdrawn after it failed to be inscribed in 2013. However, Japan has requested the Tomioka Silk Mill and Related Industrial Heritage sites for 2014. Additional cultural heritage sites include: Hikone Castle in Shiga Prefecture, Mozu-Furuichi Kofungun in Osaka, Asuka-Fujiwara in Nara Prefecture, Churches and Christian Sites in Nagasaki, Sado Gold Mines in Niigata Prefecture and Jomon Archeological Sites in the Tohoko region.

Answer the questions in complete sentences.
(1) What happened to Kamakura?

Answer each question with your own opinion.
(2) What other places do you think should be considered as a World Heritage site candidate in Japan?
(3) Which of the candidates do you think should be listed as a World Heritage site? Why do you think so? Talk about it with your partner.

著者

吉田国子（よしだ　くにこ）

日高正司（ひだか　まさし）

Harry Kearns（ハリー・カーンス）

山本　梓（やまもと　あずさ）

CD付
リスニング・スキルアップ：日本の世界遺産を巡る

2014年 4 月20日　第1版発行
2022年 9 月20日　第7版発行

| | |
|---|---|
| 著　者 | 吉田国子 |
| | 日高正司 |
| | Harry Kearns |
| | 山本　梓 |
| 発行者 | 前田俊秀 |
| 発行所 | 株式会社三修社 |
| | 〒150-0001　東京都渋谷区神宮前2-2-22 |
| | TEL 03-3405-4511 |
| | FAX 03-3405-4522 |
| | 振替 00190-9-72758 |
| | https://www.sanshusha.co.jp |
| | 編集担当　菊池　暁 |
| 印刷所 | 広研印刷株式会社 |

CD 録音　　ELEC
CD 制作　　高速録音株式会社
ブックデザイン　木ノ下 努［VERY & Co.］
編集協力　　山本 拓

© 2014 Printed in Japan ISBN978-4-384-33443-2 C1082

JCOPY〈出版者著作権管理機構 委託出版物〉

本書の無断複製は著作権法上での例外を除き禁じられています。複製される場合は、そのつど事前に、出版者著作権管理機構（電話 03-5244-5088 FAX 03-5244-5089 e-mail: info@jcopy.or.jp）の許諾を得てください。